Mount Cook

The Basin

The Basin

AN ILLUSTRATED HISTORY
OF THE BASIN RESERVE

Don Neely & Joseph Romanos

CANTERBURY UNIVERSITY PRESS

TE WHARE WĀNANGA O WAITAHA

**UNIVERSITY OF
CANTERBURY**
CHRISTCHURCH · NEW ZEALAND

First published in 2003 by
CANTERBURY UNIVERSITY PRESS
University of Canterbury
Private Bag 4800
Christchurch
NEW ZEALAND

mail@cup.canterbury.ac.nz
www.cup.canterbury.ac.nz

ISBN 1-877257-05-2

Printed by Wyatt & Wilson Print Limited, Christchurch, New Zealand

Cover: Painting by Jeremy Bennett of the Basin Reserve, based on a postcard printed in 1895.
The Mount Cook Barracks tower over the Caledonian Grandstand.

DON NEELY COLLECTION

Front endpaper: View of Wellington, September 1841. This watercolour by Charles Heaphy
was painted from Clay Point, which is behind Stewart Dawsons on the corner of Willis
Street and Lambton Quay. Mount Victoria, Mount Albert and Mount Cook,
indicated in the skyline, drained into the Basin.

ALEXANDER TURNBULL LIBRARY

Back endpaper: Drawing done in 1907 by Wellington builder G. E. Humphries and submitted
to the Wellington City Council. Humphries suggested raising the level of the Basin Reserve by
10 feet, the extra height to be used for the provision of shops and other amenities underneath
the playing surface, with the entrance at road level. His idea was that the trams should run
underground between Kent Terrace and Adelaide Road.
Humphries placed a grandstand on the eastern side of the reserve to capture the sun. Other
features were a causeway over Buckle Street and an underground shooting gallery.
Many of his ideas, so revolutionary a century ago, are now to be seen in various sports and
shopping complexes around the world and have been incorporated as a means of countering
traffic problems.

WELLINGTON CITY ARCHIVES

Title page: Looking across the Basin Reserve to St Mark's Church and Wellington College,
from an 1889 watercolour by Christopher Aubrey.

WELLINGTON COLLEGE ARCHIVES

CONTENTS

ACKNOWLEDGEMENTS

A book covering as much history and as many activities as this one could not have been written without the help of many people and we would like to acknowledge all the assistance we have been given.

A long list of people we wish to thank begins with Sir Ron Brierley, Frank Cameron, Paul Cameron, Walter Hadlee, Peter Heidenstrom, Sir Robert Jones, Trevor Rigby, Richie Romanos, Peter Sellers, Bryan Waddle, Garry Ward, Bernie Wood and Spiro Zavos. A large amount of the information contained in the book came from the extended interviews we conducted with these people, who had deep knowledge of specific aspects of the Basin's history. These interviews were later passed on to the Oral History section of the Ministry for Culture and Heritage.

Others who helped in various ways were: John Blackwell, Pete Bonner, Neil Breingan, Pauline Carmody, Dick Britten-den, Donal Duthie, Robin Fordham, Keith Gibson, Wilf Haskell, Brother Gerard Hogg, Dan Kelly, Michael Kelly, Peter Kerridge, Tom Larkin, Julia Millen, Felicity and Richard Peters, Coleen Pobar, Keith Quinn, Ian Robertson, Haydn Sherley, Graeme Sole, Steve Stevens, Jim Sullivan, Grant Tilly, David Tossman, Spencer Wade, Geoff Watson and Barbara Yaldwyn. Thank you to you all.

We went to several libraries and groups for assistance, especially in our search for photographs. Joan McCracken, John Sullivan and Marion Minson at the Alexander Turnbull Library did all they could for us. So did Paddianne Neely, whose access to the archives at Wellington College, Wellesley College and Scots College produced a number of gems. Peter Wood of the Order of St John and Wendy Leahy of the St Patrick's College Wellington Archives were extremely helpful. Other illustrations came from St Mark's Archives, the Archdiocesan Archives, the City of Wellington Highland Pipe Band, Wellington Soccer Association, the Wellington City Archives, the IHC Archives, Agenda and the New Zealand Cricket Museum.

Information came from several publications. Newspapers and magazines referred to were: *The Dominion, Evening Post, New Zealand Free Lance, New Zealand Times, Sports Post, New Zealand Colonist, Sports Digest, Independent, Weekly News, New Zealand Listener* and *New Zealand Graphic*.

Finally we wish to thank our publisher, Canterbury University Press, editor Richard King and office manager Kaye Godfrey.

Books that contained valuable information were:
100 Summers, Don Neely, Moa, 1975
A Century of Great New Zealand Cricketers, Joseph Romanos, Bateman, 1993
An Association with Soccer, Tony Hilton and Barry Smith, NZFA, 1991
Athletes of the Century, Peter Heidenstrom, GP, 1992
Bragge's Wellington and the Wairarapa, William Main, Millwood Press, 1976
Clarrie Grimmett, Ashley Mallett, University of Queensland Press, 1993
Cricket Across the Seas, Pelham Warner, Longmans, 1903
Early Wellington, Louis E Ward, Southern Reprints, 1928
Kiwis With Gloves On, Brian O'Brien, A.H. & A. W. Reed, 1960
Marching Down Under, NZ Marching Association, 1984
Marching Down Under – Supplement, NZ Marching Association, 2000
Men in White, Don Neely, Richard King and Francis Payne, Moa, 1986
More Wellington Days, Pat Lawlor, Whitcombe and Tombs, 1962
New Zealand Sporting Records and Lists, Joseph Romanos, Hodder Moa Beckett, 2001
No Bugles No Drums, Peter Snell and Garth Gilmour, Minerva, 1965
Old Wellington Days, Pat Lawlor, Whitcombe and Tombs, 1959
Old Wellington Hotels, Pat Lawlor, Millwood Press, 1974
Rugby League Annual of New Zealand, Bernie Wood, various editions
Standing in the Sunshine, Sandra Coney, Penguin Books, 1993
The New Zealand Cricket Encyclopedia, Lynn McConnell and Ian Smith, Moa Beckett, 1993
The Streets of My City, F. L. Irvine-Smith, A.H. & A. W. Reed, 1948
The Summer Game, Don and Paddianne Neely, Moa Beckett, 1994
The Visitors, Rod Chester and Neville McMillan, Moa, 1990
The Way We Were, text Valerie Davies, Moa Beckett, 1994
Those Were the Days, compiled by Stephen Barnett, Moa, various editions
Wellington, Pat Lawlor, Millwood Press, 1976

PREFACE

THE BASIN RESERVE, situated so close to the centre of Wellington, is arguably the most famous sports ground in New Zealand. It is certainly the only one that has been granted National Heritage Place status.

Since it was created by a major earthquake in 1855, it has been constantly reshaped, modernised and renovated. Through all that time, it has remained one of the major landmarks in the capital city. Visitors to Wellington, making their way from the airport to the city, drive around the Basin Reserve. So do many thousands of commuters daily as they travel to and from the capital's southern and eastern suburbs.

The Basin, as it is affectionately known, has been one of New Zealand's main international cricket venues for well over a century, and has hosted international rugby union, rugby league, soccer, hockey, athletics, boxing, basketball, synchronised swimming, Australian rules football, softball and marching. In addition, cycling, wrestling, woodchopping, lacrosse and many other sports have been played at the ground.

Besides all the sport that has taken place at the ground, the Basin has also been the venue for events as diverse as the 1945 VE Day celebrations, the 1908 Dominion Day activities, Archbishop Redwood's Diamond Jubilee gathering in 1934, Father Patrick Payton's prayer meeting in front of 25,000 people in 1953, numerous band displays, Maori carnivals in 1900 and 1903, the Concert in the Park featuring Dame Malvina Major in 1994, and a display of ballooning in 1899 by Captain Lorraine, 'the king of parachutists'. Most incredible of all was the soccer match played at night in 1878. Not only was this the first floodlit sports event in New Zealand, but it was the country's first substantial public demonstration of electric lighting.

The Basin itself is a cause of fascination, but equally, so are its neighbours, including the Mount Victoria tunnel, the Mount Cook Barracks, the Carillon, Wellington College, St Mark's Church, St Patrick's College, St Joseph's School, Wellington East Girls' College, Wellington High School (the old Technical College), the Boys' Institute, the Caledonian Hotel, Government House and the Dominion Museum.

We are both confirmed Wellingtonians for whom the Basin Reserve holds special affection and have long felt that the story of this remarkable ground needed to be told. The challenge was to present the story in an attractive and entertaining way – hence the decision to make it an illustrated history.

Don Neely and Joseph Romanos
February 2003

ONE

Reflections – Sir Ron Brierley

Sɪʀ Rᴏɴ Bʀɪᴇʀʟᴇʏ has been one of the pivotal figures in the history of the Basin Reserve over the past half-century. He grew up in Island Bay and attended Island Bay Primary School. 'I had a tenuous early connection with the Basin in 1947,' Brierley recalls. 'Our school cricket team was permitted to go to the Basin to see the great Walter Hammond bat for England. I was very unhappy that I wasn't in the team, and derived some satisfaction because Hammond got out cheaply!'

Brierley was a confirmed cricket lover even before he attended Wellington South Intermediate and, from 1951 to 1954, Wellington College. 'I spent many happy hours at the Basin as a young boy. Christmas Day was always a special – first-class cricket began at 2 p.m. and there would be two sessions of play. In the 1948–49 season, I went along to watch Auckland play Wellington

and saw Don Taylor dismissed with the first ball of game. Seeing Plunket Shield cricket at the Basin was a great treat in those days. One game I loved was the trial match before the 1949 team to England was picked. I sat in old stand at the media table and scored the whole game. The top 22 players in New Zealand played, so it was a real thrill for me.

'Gramophone records were played over loudspeaker during breaks. I recall "Water, Water, Cool, Clear Water", sung by the Sons of the Pioneers, and still think of the Basin when I hear that country and western song. I also associate the Basin with gas cooking, from the little kiosk there, and liquorice toffees, which were sold in a shop across the road from the ground. There used to be quite a row of shops across from the Basin, at the northern end of the ground. A fish-and-chip shop there was particularly popular.'

Other memories for the young Brierley include seeing famous England player Joe Hardstaff playing for

Auckland at the Basin. 'He and Merv Wallace batted beautifully that day. Hardstaff made 81 and Wallace 113. The Basin was my home ground, and I have great memories of the place. It had such a lot of character and we are lucky so much of the original Basin has been preserved while the ground has been modernised.'

Before the 1952 cricket season, there was some wonderful news for Brierley. 'Bernie Paetz, the master in charge of cricket at Wellington College, asked me and another boy to become scoreboard attendants at the Basin for senior and for first-class cricket. This was a very important moment in my life. It gave me an official pass to the Basin, a treasured item, and on top of that I was paid 10 shillings per match. My appointment coincided with the upgrading and repainting of the scoreboard. That first season was extraordinary – there was a succession of wet Saturdays, so there was virtually no club cricket before Christmas.'

The young lads who were scoreboard attendants back then took their lives into their hands. Regular Basin cricket patrons with a longish memory will recall the large metal plates that were used to spell out names and to signal numbers on the board. On windy days those flying metal plates were a danger to all within close range, and particularly the boys on the scoreboard.

'It was dangerous work,' says Brierley. 'The ladder went directly up, at no angle. When the winds got up, it became difficult to lean across to change numbers and neither of us boys would go to the top on windy days.'

Brierley was on the scoreboard on 7 January 1952, when John Reid plundered 283 for Wellington against Otago. Reid kept the boys busy that day, as he smashed 41 boundaries and a six. 'At 150, he hit a ball straight up in the air and was dropped. So in a way he played two innings. Reid always kept us busy. We used to do the score in 10s or at the end of each over.'

A week earlier, Brierley had made his scoreboard 'debut' during a remarkable Wellington v. Central Districts match that apparently ended in a tie when the final Central batsman, Arthur Cresswell, was run out. Central, set 214 to win, had totalled 213 – according to the scoreboard – and the players headed for the pavilion believing the thrilling match had been tied.

A painting by Rodger Harrison of the new Basin Reserve was presented to the Marylebone Cricket Club to mark the club's 200th year. Rob Vance, who was in London attending an International Cricket Conference meeting in July 1984, made the presentation.

But there was plenty of drama to follow. One of the umpires, Jock McLellan, discovered when checking the scorebooks that a no-ball he had signalled did not appear in the extras. The score was amended and Central were declared winners by one wicket.

Brierley, even in these early years, was meticulous with figures (a trait that was to stand him in good stead during his business career) and is emphatic to this day that the declared result was incorrect. 'Harry Hatch and Ernie Ketko were the scorers for that game,' he says. 'Harry, it would be fair to say, was the senior partner.

He could be very dogmatic, and tended to have a short fuse. Ernie was a milder man. On the scoreboard we became attuned to knowing what was happening. After each over a scorer would call out how many runs had been scored off it. But we got to the stage where we knew anyhow, without help from the scorers.

The Basin Reserve scoreboard on the lovely summer's day when John Reid set a record for the highest score for Wellington. The scoreboard had been repainted at the start of the 1952–53 season.

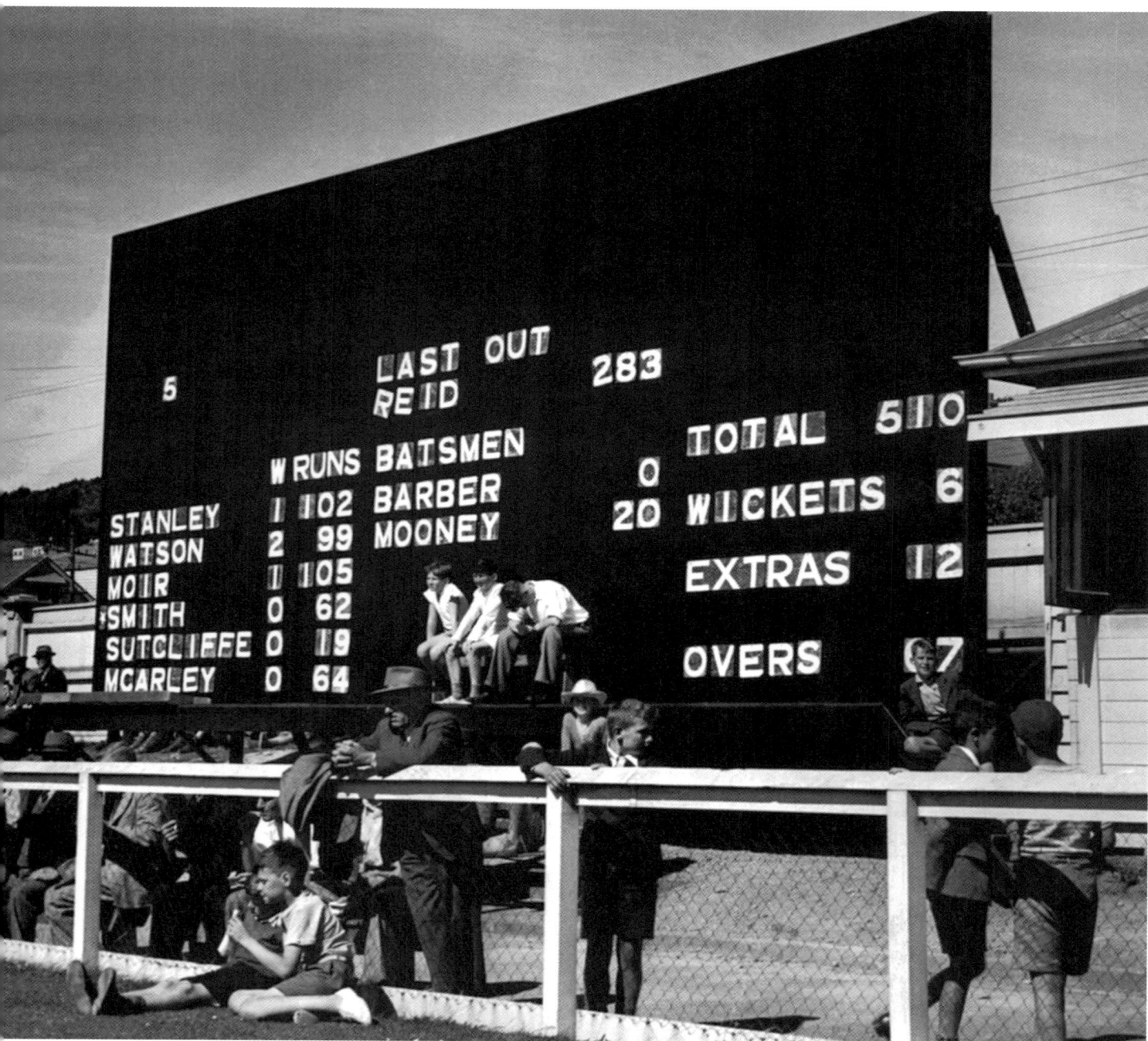

'As the game got more and more exciting, mistakes were made inside that scorebox. By the end of the match, Harry was so flustered no-one would ever know what really happened. There was chaos and confusion. Neither the board nor the books bore relation to reality.'

During club cricket, the boys would score only the game on the No. 2 pitch, the more eastern of the two. 'Though we scored only one match, it was always extra exciting having two games to keep track of. One day Trevor Barber made 254 for Wellington College Old Boys against Karori in a club match on the other wicket.'

A disappointment for Brierley during his scoreboard career was that he never got to work a test match. 'This was a plum job and there was some politics involved in the selection of attendants for those matches. In addition, test matches seemed to be held during school time.'

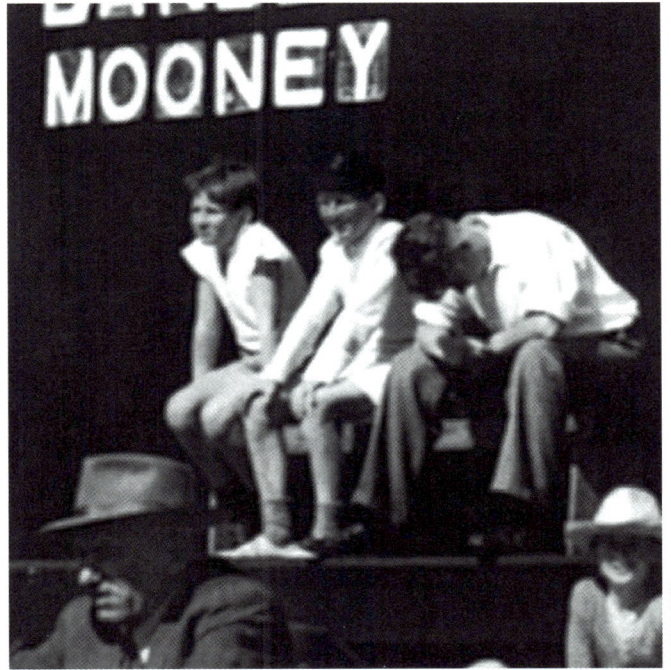

Three young lads seem to be enjoying their scoreboard duties. The boy in the middle is Ron Brierley. On his right is his brother Ken and on his left is Neil Breingan.

THE LIFE OF BRIERLEY

As one of those who grew up with Ron Brierley, I particularly enjoyed reminiscing with 'A capitalist childhood' (November 5).

One incident, referred to briefly, was memorable. In the early 1950s, Ron and I had worked on the Basin Reserve scoreboard for a couple of years, including the Plunket Shield matches. We were always supplied with passes of differing colour and letter to enable us to join the players for lunch and afternoon tea. We did not always use these, so at the end of the season, we had quite a collection.

Both of us looked forward to the visit of the South African cricket team under Jack Cheetham, but for some reason the principal of Wellington College would not release us for scoreboard duties for the first test. So on the Monday after school, we rushed over to the Basin Reserve and used our passes to enter. It was afternoon-tea time and the players and officials were entering the pavilion under the old grandstand. Noting the colour and letter of the pass being used, we shuffled through our spares.

Doffing our caps and carrying our schoolbags, we presented our passes to a sceptical doorman and entered. We sat at one of the tables with a couple of cricketers, and looked around to take stock. Horror of horrors! There, sitting at the head table was the new Governor-General, Sir Willoughby Norrie. We had gate-crashed the Vice-Regal reception.

We managed to control our panic and avoid the glares of the officials at the head table. Reasoning that the Governor-General and entourage would leave through the front doors, we would make our escape by negotiating the changing-room corridors, leave by the players' entrance, and be home free. We didn't quite make it. The President and Secretary of the Wellington Cricket Association, wise to our plan, must have taken hasty leave of Sir Willoughby and rushed to cut us off. The scene that followed was frightful.

Neil Breingan
(Stoke)

This letter, written by one of Brierley's best mates at school, was published in the *New Zealand Listener* on 26 November 1990.

The two officials in question were Norman Chapman, the Wellington association secretary, and Harold Osborne, the chairman. Ironically, Brierley and Osborne were to open the batting for many years for the Midland second-grade team. Rob Vance, chairman of the Wellington Cricket Association and later the New Zealand Cricket Council, and a long-time friend of Brierley, used to regurgitate the incident annually, with great relish.

BASKETBALL

Sponsored by the *Coca-Cola* Export Corporation

BASIN RESERVE
JANUARY 16 and 17

ABE SAPERSTEIN'S
Fabulous

HARLEM
GLOBETROTTERS

30th SEASON

WELLINGTON BOXING ASSOCIATION (Incorp.)
NEW ZEALAND

SOUVENIR
PROGRAMME

BRITISH EMPIRE
WELTERWEIGHT
CHAMPIONSHIP

Gerald Dreyer v. Barry Brown

SOUTH AFRICA
CHAMPION

NEW ZEALAND
CONTENDER

15 3-MINUTE ROUNDS

BASIN RESERVE – JANUARY 15, 1954
First Gong 8 p.m.

Official Programme 2/6

AMERICAN
ALL STARS

V.

WELLINGTON

BASIN RESERVE – AUGUST 8, 1953

1/- SOUVENIR PROGRAMME 1/-

RUGBY LEAGUE

Aztec Services Pty. Ltd.
proudly presents

WORLD'S GREATEST
WATER & STAGE SHOW

SAM SNYDER'S
Internationally Famous
WATER
FOLLIES

AUSTRALASIAN TOUR 1957
OFFICIAL SOUVENIR PROGRAM

The 1950s was an exciting time to be growing up near the Basin Reserve. Not only was there cricket in the summer and soccer in the winter (Brierley has especially fond memories of the famous Petone Settlers' run to the Chatham Cup title in 1949), but there was a vast variety of other events held at the Basin. These included the American All Stars gridiron team playing a rugby league match against Wellington in 1953; the first British Empire boxing title fight held in New Zealand, Barry Brown v. Gerald Dryer in 1954; the visit by the Harlem Globetrotters in 1957; and the Water Follies exhibition the same year.

During the winters, Brierley continued to look after the scoreboard. 'I was the sole scoreboard attendant for soccer. I'd do early game by the scoreboard and used to get paid two shillings. After the game, I'd put the letters and numbers away and catch the tram back to Island Bay. I may even have done a rugby league match or two.'

After graduating from the scoreboard, Brierley played cricket in the lower grades for Midland, often accompanying the club on its Christmas tours, and then went on to stamp his mark on the world of commerce. He recalls vividly the last time he played for Midland. 'It was in 1983 and Midland held their reunion at the Basin. It was the only time I played on the main wicket. It was an interesting experience being out in the centre. I was surprised how close stands were.'

In the 1950s, there wasn't much variety of entertainment available and a band display at the Basin was an inviting proposition. A packed crowd braves the brisk weather to spend the afternoon watching a succession of Wellington's leading bands. St Patrick's College looks somewhat forbidding in the background. Reaching into the sky are a Basin Reserve lighting tower and the Bryant and May factory chimneys.
DAVID TOSSMAN

Even as he climbed the business ladder, cricket, and the Basin, remained close to Brierley's heart. He has been a regular attender at big cricket matches all over the world, but makes no secret of the fact that Basin Reserve tests are always special for him.

A match that looms very large occurred in 1978, when New Zealand beat England for the first time. 'There was a howling wind and Bob Willis bowled a fierce first over. I think John Wright may have been fortunate to be given the benefit of the umpire's doubt off the first ball of the match. It was a very unpromising start to the game. But five days later it had become one of the most memorable ever at the Basin.'

Among his more recent highlights have been the tests against England in 1984, and against Sri Lanka in 1991.

'Jeremy Coney made 174 against England, his maiden test century. He batted exceptionally well that day. As Martin Crowe also made a century and Lance Cairns held out for a long time, New Zealand was able to save the test in dramatic circumstances.'

During his 82-match test career, John Wright scored three of his 12 centuries at the Basin Reserve. The most enjoyable was his 117 not out in New Zealand's second innings against Australia in March, 1990.

Wright and his New Zealand team-mates celebrated their nine-wicket win afterwards in their Basin Reserve dressing room. From left: Wright (holding the Trans-Tasman Trophy), Martin Crowe, Mark Greatbatch, Ken Rutherford, Richard Hadlee, Jeff Crowe, Ian Smith.

DON NEELY COLLECTION

The Basin Reserve usually provided rich pickings for New Zealand's greatest cricketer, Richard Hadlee. It was the only ground where he had two 10-wicket hauls in test matches.

Hadlee announced his arrival as a world-class bowler by taking 7–23 in India's second innings at the Basin in 1976, and his last test at home took place at the same ground, against Australia in 1990. New Zealand won both matches in emphatic fashion.

His most memorable day at the ground came in February 1986, when he had Australian captain Allan Border lbw to become just the sixth bowler to claim 300 test wickets. Hadlee left no-one at the ground in any doubt that he felt he had trapped Border in front. Slips Martin Crowe and Jeremy Coney supported the champion bowler, and umpire Fred Goodall raised his finger to send Border packing – and didn't lower it until the batsman was well on his way to the pavilion.

Aravinda da Silva made a big double century for Sri Lanka in 1991 and looked to have set up his team for a win, only to see New Zealand fight back. 'Martin Crowe batted magnificently and had a world record stand with Andrew Jones to save the game. Crowe's innings ended dramatically when he was out for 299, having taken from da Silva after only a couple of days the record for the highest test score made at the Basin Reserve.'

Sir Ron – he was knighted in 1988 for his services to business management and the community – has been a munificent benefactor to Wellington cricket in many ways, ranging from helping pay for the reunions of various teams during tests at the Basin, to gifting a considerable sum to help set up the indoor cricket school at the WestpacTrust Stadium, to assisting with the setting up and purchase of exhibits for the New Zealand Cricket Museum at the Basin.

His contribution was recognised when the offices of Wellington cricket were relocated to the Basin early in 2002 in what is now known as the Sir Ron Brierley Pavilion. Sir Ron has been a president of both Wellington and New Zealand Cricket and is a life member of Cricket Wellington.

Wellington has indeed been fortunate to have as generous a patron as Sir Ron Brierley.

Sir Ron Brierley at the Basin. No-one has enjoyed watching cricket more at the ground.

TWO

An Act of God
1839–1880

THE BASIN RESERVE has been a part of Wellington for almost as long as the town has existed. Any history of the Basin runs parallel to the development of New Zealand's capital city itself. Over the past 160 years, Wellington has been developed, reshaped, redesigned and rebuilt. So has the Basin.

Wellington was the first settlement of the New Zealand Company, which was created by Edward Gibbon Wakefield. One of his five brothers, Colonel William Wakefield, acted as the company's agent, and it was he who chose the spot where Wellington now stands.

Sport and recreation were the last consideration of the New Zealand Company. In the town plan of Wellington, drawn up by the Surveyor-General, Captain William Mein Smith, there were 1,100 town allotments, but no space was provided for recreational activities. The tops of the steep hills were designated as the 'Town Belt'. Governor William Hobson, in an 1841 dispatch, noted that 'in laying out and disposing of the town allotments, there has been no attention whatsoever paid to the selection of reserves for public purposes'.

Linked to the harbour by a stream was a lagoon that Captain Smith named 'Basin', intending it to be used as a safe haven for ships. He envisaged that, as the settlement grew, the stream could be widened into a canal, used by horse-drawn barges. Warehouses would be built around the Basin, which was sited centrally to service both the city and Newtown, potentially a major residential area.

The northern streets that bordered the Basin were named Buckle and Ellice after two of the directors of the New Zealand Company. The east and west streets – Sussex Square – were named after the Duke of Sussex, whose tenuous link to Wellington was that he attended farewell dinners given by the New Zealand Company to departing emigrants. In 1912, the eastern street was renamed Dufferin Street to honour Governor-General Lord Plunket's wife, daughter of the Marquis of Dufferin. The western street later became Sussex Street. The southern street was initially named Dock Street but was soon to become Rugby Street.

Sport in England was in its infancy when Wellington's first emigrants left Gravesend on 13 September 1839, on the *Aurora*. There was pugilism, horse-racing, cock-fighting, dice and cricket – contests that appealed to the aristocracy, who would gamble on the outcome. On 20 January 1840 (now Wellington's Anniversary Day),

Part of a letter written in March 1840 by J. H. Wallace, one of the earliest Wellington colonists: '. . . the settlers went on cheerfully with the "heroic work of colonization". Shooting pigeons and ducks, which were plentiful, formed a portion of the outdoor exercises, and at Petone quoits, cricket and rifle matches [were played].'

Captain William Mein Smith was engaged by the New Zealand Company as its Surveyor-General, and he arrived at Port Nicholson on 5 January 1840, just 16 days before the first settlers. He and three assistants laid out two towns, at Petone and Thorndon. Smith also conducted the ballot for 1,100 town sections in July and August at Dicky Barrett's Hotel.

169 New Zealand Company settlers stepped ashore at Petone Beach with their meagre personal possessions, plus muskets, Bibles, oak seedlings and cricket gear.

By 1842, it was estimated that, excluding Maori and military forces and their families, the population of New Zealand was 10,992, of whom 3,701 lived in the Wellington Provincial District.

Once the rudimentary necessities of life had been provided for in the first settlements, the colonists would

Detail from Captain Smith's Wellington town plan, produced on 14 August 1840. Mount Victoria is at the top of the plan, above Smith's 'Proposed Canal and Basin', near Mount Cook.

gather to celebrate hard-earned holidays with sports meetings, which quickly became part of the colonial town's social life.

The first record of a cricket match in Wellington was 28 December 1842. Two teams from the Wellington club played a match on a ground at the Te Aro flat. The *New Zealand Colonist* reported: 'The day being remarkably fine, a considerable number of persons attended to view the game.' The Blues beat the Reds by 126 notches to 124, and a belated Christmas dinner was held at the Ship's Hotel. At this time, there were only 251 dwellings and shops in the 18,000-acre settlement.

Through the 1840s and early 1850s, Wellington made good progress as a developing town. People willing to

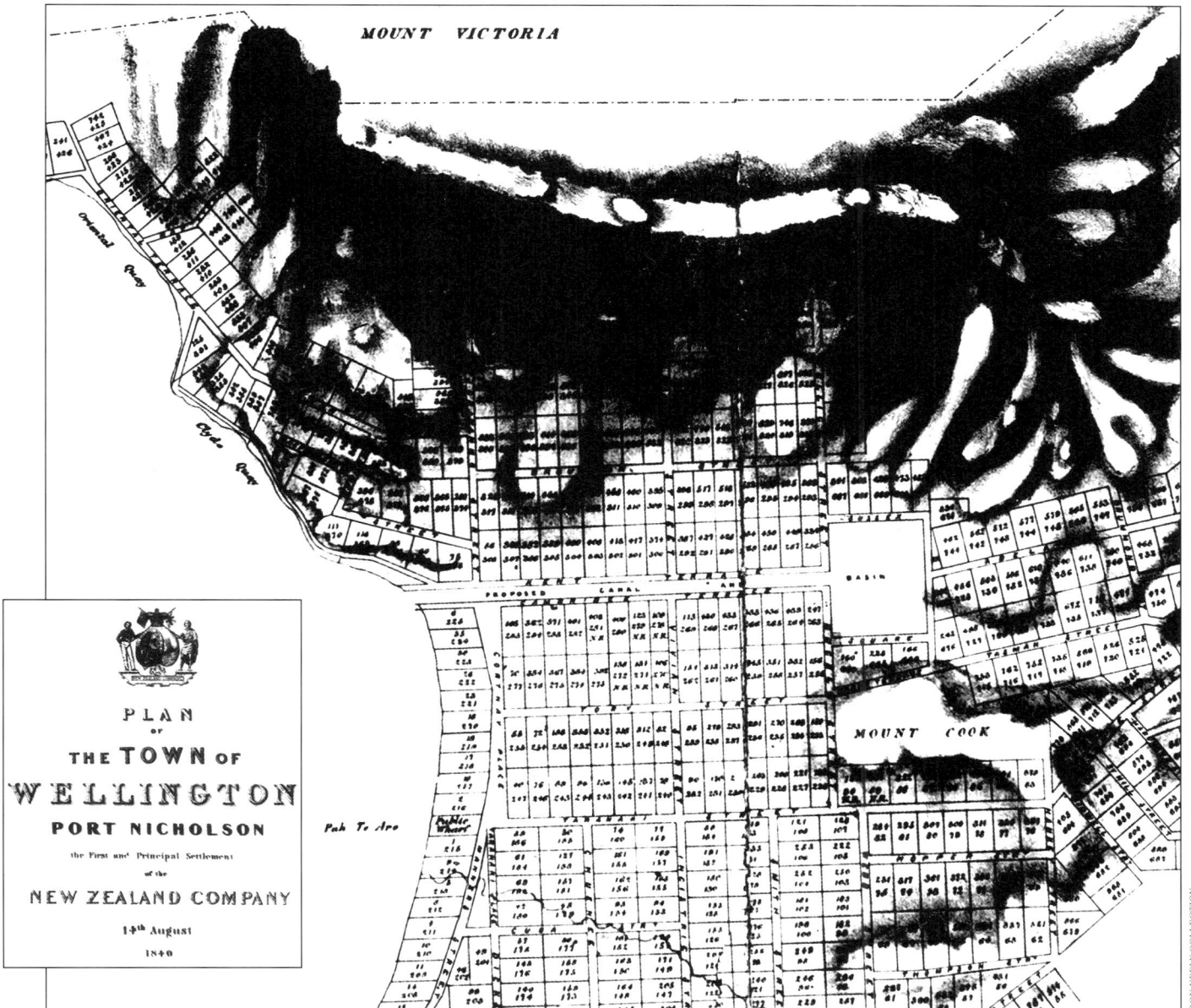

It Happened In New Zealand — By Ross Gore

FOUNDING A SETTLEMENT.

1. JANUARY 22 IS **WELLINGTON'S** ANNIVERSARY DAY, FOR ON THAT DAY, IN 1840, THE *AURORA* LANDED 169 SETTLERS AT **PETONE** BEACH;·:·BRITANNIA.

THE ADVANCE PARTY, UNDER **COL.WM·WAKE-FIELD**, HAD ARRIVED IN THE *TORY* IN 1839.

† THE SAME YEAR THE SETTLEMENT WAS RENAMED WELLINGTON IN HONOUR OF THE "IRON DUKE!"

2. THE SETTLERS IMMEDIATELY TOOK UP LAND & STARTED TO BUILD HOMES. MORE SHIPS ARRIVED & BY THE FIRST

WGTON. FROM PETONE, 1840, NEAR PRESENT RAILWAY RAMP.

ANNIVERSARY, JAN. 22, 1841, THE POPULATION WAS 2,500, OCCUPYING SOME 18,000 ACRES OF RURAL LAND.

3. THESE PIONEERS WERE MEN & WOMEN OF ENTERPRISE & ENERGY.

WOMEN PERFORMED WONDERS ESTABLISHING COMFORTABLE HOMES UNDER THE MOST PRIMITIVE CONDITIONS.

4. THE MEN INTRODUCED CIVILISED AMENITIES TO THE NEW SETTLEMENT.

IN ONE SHORT YEAR THEY HAD ALREADY PRODUCED † A NEWSPAPER,

† "THE NEW ZEALAND GAZETTE" SAMUEL REVANS, PUBLISHER.

5. AND, JUST TO SHOW THAT THEY WERE **BRITISH** TO THE BACKBONE, THEY HAD

FORMED A CRICKET CLUB,

6. BUT, LIKE TRUE **NEW ZEALANDERS**, THEY HAD ALSO HELD THEIR FIRST RACE MEETING, ANNIVERSARY DAY, 1841, & ESTABLISHED NO

LESS THAN TEN HOTELS, 5 IN **WGTON.** & 5 IN **PETONE.** WITH A POPULATION OF ONLY 2,500 TO TEN HOTELS DRINKING WAS NO DOUBT MORE CIVILISED THAN IT IS TODAY. *ROSS GORE COPYRIGHT.*

Ross Gore's series *It Happened In New Zealand* illustrates how, even in 1840, wherever British settlers ventured, cricket inevitably followed.

travel across the world for the chance to forge a better life must have been imbued with a sense of adventure, and no doubt this made Wellington an exciting place to be at that time. However, at 9.11 p.m. on 23 January 1855, the planning that had gone into the settlement's growth was turned upside down by a major earthquake, since estimated as likely to have registered 8 on the Richter scale. It left a lasting impression on Wellington and its settlers, and drastically altered the lie of the land occupied by the Basin.

Commander Drury, of HMS *Pandora*, wrote: 'For eight hours subsequent to the first great shock, the tide approached and receded from the shore every 20 minutes, rising from eight to ten feet and receding four feet lower than the spring tides. Every half an hour, lesser shocks were accompanied by hollow sounds. Lights were seen running to and fro, from all parts of town, and evidence of consternation, combined with loud crashes.'

It was reported that on the corner of Willis and Manners Streets, a considerable opening in the road emitted a slimy mud and the main street was inundated. There was a general uplift in the harbour area, more in the east than the west. The rise was nine feet in Palliser Bay, five feet in the inner harbour area and very little in Cape Terawhiti. The perimeter of the harbour – ultimately made into the Marine Drive – was essentially founded on the uplifted platform. The whole of the flat at the Te Aro end of town was raised five feet and the Basin lagoon was turned into a swamp, putting paid to the planned canal and dock scheme.

For a town so short of flat land, this act of God turned out to be a blessing in disguise.

In 1857, a group of influential citizens, frustrated at having to continually change their ground for playing cricket because of buildings being erected, successfully petitioned the Provincial Council to set aside the proposed site for the canal and basin at Te Aro as a public park. They noted that 'the land is perfectly level and contains about eight acres and is, in the opinion of your petitioners, well-adapted for the above purposes as a place for recreation'. The Provincial Council approved the petition, thereby creating the Basin Reserve.

The population of New Zealand quadrupled in the 10 years from 1851 to 1861. Soldiers, with their families, arrived to take part in the Land Wars, and thousands of adventurers were attracted by the prospect of striking it rich in the gold fields of Central Otago, Westland and the Coromandel Peninsula. Many of these, with their families, eventually settled in Wellington, whose population in 1861 was 12,566.

Beginning on 5 February 1863, prison labour from nearby Mt Cook barracks was used to flatten and drain the Basin. They dug a wide and deep channel running north to south through the ground. A report for the management of the city's reserves in September 1863 described how the area of the Basin Reserve had, by the valuable aid of prison labour, been reclaimed from a state of impossible swamp to available and almost dry land. A public subscription, supplemented by an equal amount from the provincial government, meant the

In 1860, five years after the great earthquake reshaped Wellington, Te Aro is pictured from Mount Victoria. In the foreground is the large drain from the Basin Reserve, where Cambridge Terrace is now found.

whole of the Basin Reserve could be encircled with a railed fence and planted with thorn hedge.

On 5 October 1864, Wellington was chosen, because of its central location, to be the seat of government for the colony of New Zealand. This brought a further influx of residents, as did the fact that Maori land in the lower North Island was up for grabs.

Enthusiasm for further development of the Basin waned until 1866, when agreement was reached between a working committee of interested citizens and a sub-committee of the Board of Works. It was agreed that the reserve be leased for three years, to be used as a cricket ground at an annual rental of £25. The fences were to be kept in repair and the board would plant trees and shrubs, provided they did not interfere with the playing ground, and that horses and cattle be excluded. Thus, on 11 December 1866, the Basin Reserve formally became Wellington's home of cricket.

The first game of cricket played on the Basin was on 11 January 1868 between the Wellington Volunteers and the officers and men of HMS *Falcon*. After the game, the umpire, Bruce Wallace, apologised to the players for the bad state of the ground, with stones and thistles

causing damage to hands and fingers. At the end of the day the ball looked as if it had smallpox. There were no demonstrations on this opening day, no dinners, no banners, no music.

Like other towns in the new colony, Wellington had a Caledonian Society that organised Highland Games (including athletics, novelty races, dancing and, later, cycling and wood-chopping) and offered prize-money that attracted competitors from all around the province. It was not surprising, then, that following the cricket match in January, a deputation from the Caledonian Sports Association asked if a permanent grandstand, measuring 44 by 20 feet, could be built on the western side of the Basin. They submitted a sketch and estimated the cost to be between £250 and £300. A wooden grandstand, which also housed a custodian, was built in that year by issuing debentures of £10 each. The earnings from the grandstand were to make a fund to pay interest on the debentures.

Refreshment booths also raised money during the popular Caledonian athletics meetings. Two booths were situated in the grandstand, two in the marquees on the ground selling fruit, and there were various 'Aunt Sally' stalls.

As a youngster, Douglas Maclean was heavily involved with several sports at the Basin Reserve. He won the first bicycle race held in Wellington, at one of the earliest Caledonian Sports days. In 1870, the *Independent* reported him as the captain of the Wellington football team that played 16 assembled from HMS *Rosario*, at the Basin. The sailors won the game by a goal. This is reputedly the first account of rugby in the North Island. The newspaper commented that 'so long as the ball had to be kicked along the new made artificial ground it was well enough, but once off that part, all sorts of bogs and quagmires were encountered'.

Maclean remained a keen supporter of the Caledonian gatherings and was a major benefactor. When he was knighted in 1927 for services to farming and the community, he was the chief of the Highland Society, president of the Boxing and Wrestling Association of Hawke's Bay and president of the Navy League.

Douglas Maclean achieved local fame when he rode his penny farthing bicycle over the Rimutaka Range to Masterton, this at a time when roads were no more than tracks.

DON NEELY COLLECTION

Sir Douglas Maclean later in life.

ALEXANDER TURNBULL LIBRARY

In 1864, John Marchant (right) scored 117 for Invercargill against a country team of 15. This was probably the first century scored in New Zealand. By 1870, he had transferred to Wellington, where he was Secretary for Crown Lands. In 1871, he and three other cricketers, C. A. Knapp, N. Wells and A. H. Buchanan, were the principal campaigners in raising subscriptions for further work on the Basin Reserve. Marchant made the necessary survey and plans.

He wrote in his diary: 'The ground consisted of peaty rises and hollows covered with rushes, niggerheads here and there and other rough vegetation of a partly reclaimed swamp. In the first instance, the cricketers cut and grubbed up the coarse vegetation, levelled off the humps, filled up the hollows, cut some main drains, filled in the latter with stones and scrub, and top dressed the whole as far as funds permitted, with soil obtained by cutting into and sloping back the banks on the western side. Grass seed was then sown and we carried on the operations right up to the end of the year. The following year, 1872, we employed men from June 10 until November. With horses and drays, we carried out minor draining and returfed 900 square yards for match pitches as well as greatly improving the surface and extending the levelling and sowing of the ground on the other side of the ditch which intersected the ground.'

By now Wellington had played representative cricket

DON NEELY COLLECTION

games over 13 years, mainly against Nelson, but also against Auckland and Wanganui. On 30 November 1873, the Basin hosted the first first-class match between Wellington and Auckland, with Marchant a proud captain. On 17 March 1874, he captained Wellington to the first of only three tied matches in New Zealand, against Nelson, also at the Basin. He saved the game for his side by taking six catches and taking the last wicket – just reward for a man who worked long and hard on the Basin. Marchant became New Zealand's Surveyor-General in the first decade of the twentieth century.

ALEXANDER TURNBULL LIBRARY

The Caledonian Grandstand from Wellington College looking across to Pipitea Point, in 1874, the year the college was established on its current site. In the left foreground, Adelaide Road is sparsely populated. There are no houses on Sussex Street behind the grandstand. Kent and Cambridge Terraces are the paths leading to the harbour.

In 1870, the cricketers wanted the lease of the Basin to be extended. They were told that the offer could not be entertained, but that there was no objection to leasing to three trustees: Mr Cutts, to represent the public; George Crawford to represent the Caledonian Games Committee; and Mr Buchanan, of the Bank of Australasia, to represent the cricketers. The terms were for three years at an annual rental of £20, and the upkeep of the ground was the responsibility of the trustees.

The Basin Reserve was secured for recreational purposes in 1873 when a deed, signed by the Superintendent of the Provincial Council, vested the ground in the Wellington City Council 'for such purposes of public utility'. The deed stipulated that no thoroughfare was to be built across the ground. The following year, the ground was conveyed to the trustees to be used as a cricket and recreation ground.

A. F. Wiren, a well-known cricket historian, described the Basin of 1876 in his diary: 'It had a big open drain running through the ground. It carried a good volume of water and a few planks here and there so that people could cross it. The middle of the area nearest the pavilion was in good condition, but it did have a slope to it. It was customary to run all hits out. The grass grew lank and long, while the drain itself was a great eeling resort to the Te Aro boys.'

James Bragge, a Lambton Quay photographer, captured this image of the Basin Reserve and Caledonian Grandstand in the late 1870s. Note the bridge over the ditch in the foreground and the trees that were planted in September 1877 after much public agitation. The two wooden platforms, about 18 inches high, were used for dancing competition in the Caledonian sports. To the right is the framework of a small hut. This could have been covered with tarpaulins to give the organisers or judges protection from the weather. The two goalposts are not joined by a crossbar and thus could have been used for any of the three forms of football that were then in their infancy in New Zealand – rugby, soccer and Australian rules. The well-worn athletics track indicates that by now the Basin was being used regularly.

The band rotunda and the grandstand were built in 1868. In the following decade, a bank was built on the left and a more substantial band rotunda was erected. The groundsman, who lived in the ground floor on the left side of the stand, was paid seven shillings a week by the Wellington Cricket Association and was employed only in the summer.

ENGLISH HIGH SCHOOL

Annual Christmas Sports,

TO BE HELD ON THE

BASIN RESERVE,

On MONDAY, 16th DECEMBER, 1878.

Committee:

J. HOLLIDAY	G. TULLY	E. WIDDOP
W. TRIPE	A. BUCHANAN	C. HOLDSWORTH
	D. BUCK.	

Starter—MR. BERRY.   Judge—D. CAMERON.

PROGRAMME.

1—J. 100 YARDS FLAT RACE, all ages—S. Davis, scratch, B. Duncan, 2 yards, O. Porrit, 5 yards, G. Davis, 5 yards, J. Holmes, 4 yards, R. Staples, 5 yards
2—S. 100 YARDS FLAT RACE, all ages—J. Holliday, scratch, E. Kreeft, 5½ yards, G. Tully, 3 yards, F. Barraud, 4 yards, D. Buck, 2½ yards, H. Stock, 7 yards, E. Porter, 8 yards, J. McIntosh, 6 yards
3—J. HOP, STEP AND JUMP, all ages—J. Pyke, S. Davis, B. Duncan
4—S. 100 YARDS RACE, under 15—J McIntosh, scratch, A Cameron, ¼ yard, E Widdop, ¼ yard, E Stock, 3 yards, T Cameron, 5 yards, A Wren, 2½ yards, H Stock, ½ yard, — Porter, ½ yard, W Meek, 5 yards, A Collins, ½ yard, E Ellaby, 1 yard
5—J. 440 YARDS FLAT RACE, all ages—S Davis scratch, W Pyke, 6 yards
6—S. WALKING RACE, half-mile, all ages—— Tully, scratch, A Cameron, 10 yards, T Cameron, 25 yards, A Cleland, 25 yards
7—S. 220 YARDS FLAT RACE, all ages—J Holliday, scratch, D. Buck, 2 yards, G. Tully, 4 yards, F. Barraud, 5 yards, E. Kreeft, 6 yards, E. Stock, 10 yards, A Cameron, 8 yards, T. Cameron, 12 yards, H. Stock, 8 yards, E. Ellaby, 8½ yards, E Porter, 9 yards, J McIntosh, 7 yards
8—J. 220 YARDS FLAT RACE, all ages—S Davis, scratch, W Pyke, 4 yards, B Duncan, 4 yards, G Davis, 7 yards, O Porritt, 7 yards, J Holme, 6 yards
9—S. HALF-MILE FLAT RACE, all ages—J Holliday, scratch, G Tully, 5 yards, D Buck, 1 yard, F. Barraud, 10 yards, E. Stock, 23 yards, E. Kreeft, 15 yards, A Cameron, 20 yards, T Cameron, 30 yards, H Stock, 20 yards, E Porter, 23 yards
10—J. HALF-MILE WALKING RACE, all ages—S Davis, scratch, J Pyke, 10 yards
11—S. ONE HUNDRED YARDS FLAT RACE, under 16—E. Kreeft, scratch, J McIntosh, ½-yard, A Cameron, 1 yard, T Cameron, 5 yards, H Stock, 1 yard, J E Porter, 3 yards, A Collins, 3 yards, E. Ellaby 2 yards
12—J. 100 YARDS FLAT RACE, under 12—G Davis, scratch, O Porritt, scratch, R Staples, 2 yards, A Meek, 5 yards, G Shennon, 6 yards
13—S. 440 YARDS FLAT RACE, all ages—J Holliday, scratch, D Buck, 1 yard, G Tully, 3 yards, E Kreeft, 6 yards, A Cameron, 8 yards, F Barraud, 5 yards, T Cameron, 12 yards
14—S. HURDLE RACE, 150 YARDS, 6 HURDLES, under 16—— Kreeft, scratch, H Stock, 2 yards, A Cleland, 5 yards, E Ellaby, 3 yards, E Porter, 4 yards, A Cameron, 3 yards, A Collins, 3 yards
15—J. LONG JUMP, all ages—S Davis, J Pyke, B Duncan
16—S. HURDLE RACE, 150 YARDS, all ages—J Holliday, scratch, D Buck, 2 yards, — Tully, 4 yards, E Kreeft, 6 yards, A Cameron, 7 yards
17—S. HOP, STEP, AND JUMP, all ages—G Tully, J Holliday, E Kreeft, F Barraud, D Buck
18—J. CONSOLATION RACE, 220 yards, all ages
19—S. STEEPLECHASE, about 600 yards—Holliday, scratch, D Buck, scratch, G Tully, 4 yards, F Barraud, 6 yards, A Cleland, 15 yards, E Kreeft, 7 yards, E Stock, 12 yards
20. CONSOLATION RACE, 220 yards, all ages.

A. H. BUCHANAN,
Hon. Sec.

English High School was a short-lived venture initiated by the Reverend T. A. Bowden, who was the headmaster of Wellington College when it was situated on Clifton Terrace in 1867. When the college opened at its present site in 1874, Bowden had left and opened an opposition English High School in Featherston Street. He later moved to Abel Smith Street, which ultimately became the first home of Wellington Girls' High School (now Wellington Girls' College).

▶ By 1879, the familiar neighbours of the Basin Reserve were making their appearance. From left: St Mark's Church, built in 1876, Wellington College (1874), Oliver's Caledonian Hotel (1875). The horse in the foreground was used by the groundsman for rolling cricket wickets, shifting soil and other heavy work.

Meanwhile, buildings around the Basin continued to take shape. In 1874, Sir James Fergusson, the Governor of New Zealand, was one of a committee that arranged for the purchase of Town Acre 671 from the Provincial Government as a site for a church and parsonage at a cost of £281. Bishop Hadfield consecrated the first portion of the original Church of St Mark in May 1876. Ever since, St Mark's Church and School have formed a distinctive backdrop for the many events that have occurred at the Basin, with the church spire creating a cricket scene typical of those in England.

The twentieth of July 1876 was a momentous day in the history of two great colleges, Wellington College and Nelson College, which met at the Basin in the first inter-collegiate rugby match in New Zealand, and probably the world.

The Nelson boys arrived at 8 a.m., after a rough crossing, and the teams took the field at 2.30 p.m. Wellington won by two potted goals and a try, the final score being 14–0. The match, played in calm weather, was divided into four half-hour spells and it was almost dark when the game was called off five minutes early.

Several players sported beards and side-whiskers, and the most amazing physical specimen was A. W. G. Burnes, the Wellington College captain. Burnes, who in 1875 had become the first schoolboy to represent his province at rugby, was, according to a description at the time, '. . . a full grown man, tall, active and powerful. He was very bald and wore a black bushy beard'.

Nelson supporters claimed later that but for seasickness their team would have won, and pointed to a 7–2 victory in the return match as proof of their contention.

In a letter written several years afterwards, Hubert Burnett, a member of the Nelson team, said, 'One detail very firmly fixed in my mind is that we played two men short. We tried to get Wellington to play 13 men only, without success. I expect they considered that as they allowed Mr Firth to play for us (he very recently became a Junior Master), his 16 stone would largely equalise the weights of the teams.' J. P. (Joseph) Firth was to be headmaster of Wellington College from 1892 to 1920.

Football was played regularly at the Basin and was well reported. 'The play in the football match on the Basin Reserve on Saturday [22 July 1876],' stated the *Evening Post*, 'was tolerably good, but neither side could succeed in kicking a goal. The multitude of black and yellow striped legs [the new uniform] had an exceedingly comical effect, looking like so many magnified wasps' bodies.'

It must not be forgotten that in 1877 cricket was New Zealand's national sport. Rugby union was virtually unknown, and there was little else in the way of sporting pastimes. When Lillywhite's All-England XI played a Wellington XXII in a match beginning on 5 February 1877, a general holiday was proclaimed and schools were closed on the Monday and Tuesday. After the game, Jack Selby of Nottinghamshire challenged anyone in the city to a running race. Six weeks later, this England side played Australia at the Melbourne Cricket Ground in cricket's first official test match.

LIGHTING UP THE BASIN

Friday, 5 June 1879 was a landmark day for Wellington as one of the most unusual sports events in the city's history took place. Night soccer came to Wellington. To demonstrate electric lighting to the public, a game of soccer was played at the Basin between the gentlemen of Te Aro and Thorndon. The Government Electrician, Mr Smith, set up a portable 16-horsepower engine to provide electricity for two lights, one at each end of the field.

Spectators flocked to the Basin to see the new marvel, and it was estimated that 8,000 people crowded around the fence, more than a quarter of Wellington's population at that time. The grandstand was empty, as it had been decorated with Chinese lanterns. The lighting was powerful enough, said a newspaper report the following day, for 'the red stockings of the Te Aro team to be very conspicuous'. Spectators could recognise people outside the ground and marvelled that they could see St Mark's Church and houses on the surrounding hills. The Volunteer Fire and Drum Band was engaged to play and people danced.

Mr Smith suffered several false starts when the game began after the players were photographed at 8 pm. One of the lights refused to work, so he was forced to carry one light along the sideline as play moved up and down the field. Occasionally the motor missed and the light would dim for a moment. Several times it cut out altogether, leaving the players in darkness. With the teams scoreless, the motor finally overheated and the light went out and could not be restarted. Thus ended New Zealand's first floodlit sports event and the first substantial public demonstration of electric lighting.

THREE

The Social Hub of Wellington
1881–1900

THE LAST TWO DECADES of the nineteenth century were critical for the Basin Reserve. The ground was transformed from a rough, semi-swampy paddock with a stream running through the middle into an international sports field. It was spruced up in other ways, too, with a secure fence encircling it and a bank built up on the eastern side. The surrounds of the Basin began to take shape, as well. Wellington College, St Mark's School, St Patrick's College and St Joseph's School were either built or added to. Other imposing landmarks in place by the end of this period included the Mount Cook Barracks, where the Dominion Museum was to be built in 1936, and the Caledonian Hotel.

In 1880, the population of Wellington Province was only 61,371. This had risen to 141,354 by 1900. This should be borne in mind when considering attendances for various events. In an era when there was no public transport, it was extraordinary that the Basin should often attract several thousand spectators, especially to cricket matches.

Through the 1880s, cricket had no real rival as a summer attraction. There were few places to go on a Saturday afternoon except to the Botanic Gardens and the Basin. There was no golf, tennis or bowls to speak of. Recreational cycling was a thing of the future. Arthur Lydiard's jogging revolution would not take place for another 80 years. Visits to the beach were rare; there were no motorcars to entice spectators further afield and, anyway, roads in nineteenth century Wellington were rudimentary. A trip to Karori was a serious venture, not to be undertaken lightly.

Cricket attracted spectators to the Basin not only for club and representative fixtures, but even for practices. A prominent Wellington cricketer was a local celebrity. Cricket was to remain New Zealand's national game until the early twentieth century, when New Zealand

began playing official rugby tests, and when Dave Gallaher's All Blacks embarked on their pioneering tour of Britain and France.

The Basin was far more than merely a cricket ground. Football (both soccer and rugby), cycling and athletics were often held there. In November 1889, a game of baseball was played at the Basin between Wellington and a team called Hick's Sawyer Minstrels. The ground was used for one-off events like exhibition ballooning, New Zealand's 50-year jubilee celebrations, band days and various Maori gatherings. During their lifetime, most Wellington citizens of the time would have had reason to attend events at the Basin.

By 1881, the Caledonian Society was experiencing financial worries and offered to sell the grandstand to the city council for £200. On the casting vote of the mayor, this proposal was rejected on 7 April 1881, though the following month a price of £150 was accepted. After extensive improvements by the council, the open drain was piped and covered and the area ploughed and sown with grass seed.

In June 1881, the Public Works Committee recommended that the Basin Reserve should become a pleasure park and garden, and that cricket and football be restricted to Newtown Park. The recommendation was not adopted. Football, especially, seemed to cause problems for Basin supporters. The *New Zealand Times* said in an editorial on 9 August 1881: 'The funds expended by the cricketers year after year upon the reserve had to a large amount been wasted. The cricketers paid no less than £150 per year which footballers had destroyed during the season devoted to their favourite, but decidedly dangerous sport.'

After being closed for more than a year, the ground re-opened on 7 October 1882 with a luncheon in the pavilion. This led to a surge in interest in cricket, there

An early 1880s view of the Basin Reserve from Tasman Street. The street running down the centre of the photo was known initially as Dock Street, relating to the original Wellington town plan. In 1857, its name was changed to Rugby Street, somewhat ironic because, of all the sports played at the ground over the past century and a half, rugby has not figured particularly prominently.

In front of the parsonage of St Mark's, it appears as though a flock of sheep is grazing on the Basin.

being more than 300 members, senior and junior, in nine clubs. These players were each levied 10 shillings for top-dressing and repairs, and a further five shillings for the curator and his staff of two. Senior and junior club championships were first contested in the 1883–84 season. The prize for senior champions was the Pearce Cup, named after Colonel E. Pearce, who had been the Wellington Cricket Association patron since 1875 and would so remain until 1897.

Rugby tended to be played on the Basin as pick-up matches rather than in any organised form. The council intended that Newtown Park would be the home of football as the Basin was the home of cricket. Early in the winter of 1884, a group of footballers would meet for an evening kickabout. The council endeavoured to stop them. Information was laid against one of the footballers, Bob Lynch, and a case was heard by Resident Magistrate Wardell and dismissed. The 1873 Deed of Trust was declared void. The case created great interest. The Prime Minister, Sir Robert Stout, was approached and another deed was enacted, again banning football.

Gazetted on 18 December 1884, the Deed of Conveyance of the Basin Reserve, from the Crown and Governor of New Zealand to the Wellington City Council, confirmed the recreational purpose of the ground and implied the primacy of cricket over other sports at the ground. The deed stated that the ground was to be 'forever used for purposes of cricket and recreation by the inhabitants of the city of Wellington'. This document has determined the purpose of the reserve ever since.

January 1890 was an historic time for New Zealand, as it marked the 50th jubilee of the colony. This was the first year that the entire population of Wellington – 30,000 – had been invited to participate in marking the anniversary. The Basin was a focal point for the celebrations. Sports were held there on Wednesday, 22 January, and Thursday, 23 January. Children's amusements took place on the Wednesday, and the following day there was athletics for adults. (A ham was the prize for climbing the greasy pole.) Children were not allowed to participate unless they had walked from their school to join the procession that preceded these events, then the two miles from Government Buildings to the Basin. The weather was fine, so the 14-pounder gun on Mount

Victoria was fired twice to indicate that the event was on.

It must have been a memorable occasion for the children – contemporary reports refer to each of them being given 'two sorts of cakes, six ounces each, three ounces of lollies and a gallon of liquid, such as lemonade and ginger beer'. As two hundredweight of biscuits was also distributed among them, it is a wonder they were in any condition for sport! The *Evening Post* said it was 'a spread which long abided in the memories of those who were entertained'.

The Basin's uses continued to expand as Wellington's population increased and more organisations were formed. For instance, within a few weeks in early 1894, there was club cricket and a representative cricket match between Wellington and New South Wales, in which Wellington teenager Frank Ashbolt proved to be a sensation, taking 6 wickets for 52. No sooner had the cricket finished than the Druids, the Wellington Cycling Club, a local athletics club and the Wellington harriers took over Basin.

In 1897, Councillor W. H. Barber moved that, with a view to continuing Cambridge and Kent Terraces through the Basin and widening Adelaide Road, the City Valuer be instructed to furnish a statement of the amount likely to be obtained from the sale or lease of sections of the Basin fronting Sussex Square. It was not the first, or last, time the Basin's future would be questioned at council level. On this occasion the proposal met with solid opposition, perhaps best reflected by a letter John Plimmer wrote to the *Evening Post*.

Signing himself 'The Father of Wellington', Plimmer described the 1897 transportation plan as 'greedy vandalism'. He continued: 'The Basin Reserve in the midst of the city is the people's recreation ground – the only place where women and nurses and children can retire at all times from the dirt and danger of the crowded streets.' The *New Zealand Times* entered the controversy: 'The people of Wellington will not stand idly by and permit this land to be cut up in the manner proposed. It is centrally located and by far the most popular holiday resort in the city.'

The new band rotunda, on the southern side of the Caledonian Grandstand.

DON NEELY COLLECTION

Basin Reserve Wellington. N.Z. FGR 5957

The year 1882 was notable for the erection of the oldest structure still associated with the Basin Reserve. Colonel William Wakefield, regarded as the first leader of the Wellington settlement, died in 1848 and almost immediately his friends began raising money to fund a memorial. However, it was not until 1862 that the monument – a small Corinthian temple – was ordered and shipped. Originally it was intended as a beacon at the heads, but that was superseded by the erection of the lighthouse at Pencarrow. Instead, the temple sat in Bethune and Hunter's yard until 1866 and thereafter in the Wellington City Council yard, the subject of constant debate.

Finally, in 1882, with most of those initially involved in the fundraising for the Wakefield Memorial long dead, the council decided to place the structure on the eastern side of the Basin. A drinking fountain was added.

When the temple was finally erected, the *New Zealand Times* said: 'Those who have used the subject to make merry upon will be forced to admit that it adds considerably to the beauty of the ground.' Within a few years, the Basin was fenced off and a small rise was built on the eastern side. The memorial, now with steps leading to it, was resited in the centre overlooking the reserve that Wakefield had hoped would became an inland harbour.

It remained there until 1917, when the building of a fence and the subsequent reduction in available space, meant the memorial had to be moved to a nearby site, outside the fence. Although now without its fountain and plaque, it has stayed there ever since.

The Basin Reserve photographed from Mount Victoria in 1884. Pine trees ring the ground. Overlooking the Basin on the western side is the Huston Brickworks in Wallace Street. Over the years, the crest of Mount Cook has been levelled flat with the surplus soil used for filling gullies.

The Te Aro flat and adjacent hills were largely unpopulated in 1884 when a site on the lower slopes of Mount Cook was chosen by the Marist Fathers to establish St Patrick's College. The area, bought for £3,500, ran from Buckle Street to Tui Lane. The college was opened in 1885 and remained a dominant presence, towering over the north-west corner of the Basin Reserve for the next 95 years, until the area was sold back to the city for $2.9 million to make way for a motorway extension. St Patrick's College shifted to Evans Bay in 1979.

Overshadowing the citizens of Wellington, walking in their Sunday best, the formidable Mount Cook Barracks look more like a Dickensian poor-house. During the New Zealand Wars, military barracks were built on Mount Cook to accommodate several hundred men. As the *Evening Post* reported, 'The miniature fortress was well-fitted to withstand any attack the turbulent Natives might make.'

In 1870, when the imperial forces left the colony, the barracks were used as temporary quarters for immigrants. The first Inspector of Prisons, Colonel A. Hume, a former deputy-governor of Pentonville Jail, England, suggested that the existing barracks be demolished and a huge central prison be built in their place. When it was agreed, prisoners were marched each day in chains from the Terrace Jail across the city to pull down the

barracks, then make bricks, then finally build another grim penitentiary. The surface area of Mount Cook, which had been lowered 70 feet when the barracks were built, was now lowered by another 30 feet.

The wings of the barracks comprised a basement and three storeys. The entrance at the southern end featured two towers 150 feet high. A similar wing at the northern end overlooking the city and harbour was used as offices for the staff. From the outset, there was considerable public feeling against the barracks and their dominating appearance, as they hovered over the Basin Reserve's Caledonian Grandstand.

Prime Minister Seddon told the House of Representatives in 1897 that 'a great error of judgement has been committed by the erection of a jail on the noblest site in Wellington'.

The presentation of colours to the First Battalion, Wellington Rifles, in June 1887.
The Basin Reserve certainly seemed a vast ground in the nineteenth century.

Another Sunday in the 1890s, another procession at the Basin.

▶ A female cyclist is given a helping hand at the start of her race. The occasion, a combined cycling and athletics meeting, drew an overflow crowd. Cycling had an on-and-off relationship with the Basin Reserve. In 1885, the Wellington City Council declined a request for a cycle track at the ground, but races continued to be held there until the late 1950s.

ALEXANDER TURNBULL LIBRARY

▼ March 1888 and a Wellington side of XXII takes on the English cricket team. The Basin Reserve's shape makes it almost unrecognisable. It appears to be a massive, elongated, sprawling park, not the tightly enclosed oval it has become. Note that three of the visiting English fieldsmen are wearing jackets and that the umpires are in dark suits. A spire is being added to St Mark's Church.

NEW ZEALAND CRICKET MUSEUM

The Basin Reserve has seldom been used for major rugby matches but was the venue for two big fixtures in May 1888. On the 12th, Great Britain and Wellington drew 3-3, and two days later the visitors beat Harry Roberts's XV by 4–1. Bob Seddon, who lost his life in a sculling accident when the team moved on to the Australian leg of their tour, captained the tourists. There was a cricket flavour to the rugby team because crack centre Andrew Stoddart was the touring team's player-manager. He was an even more outstanding cricketer, a brilliant batsman and a successful England cricket captain. He is the only person to have captained England at both cricket and rugby.

The Wellington team included famous players Davy Gage, Joe Warbrick, Tom Ellison and Sammy Cockroft. The match drew 7,000 spectators, who watched as the visitors led 3–0 at halftime and were overjoyed when local centre Thomson drop-kicked a goal in the second half to level the scores.

It was recorded that a 'stylish young half-caste lady' was so carried away that she called out from the pavilion, 'Kill 'em all, Wellington, kill 'em all.' But Wellington did no such thing; they played two men short for much of the match and did well to force a draw.

The second match, hastily arranged when a Great Britain v. Wairarapa fixture fell through, was played in a thick southerly drizzle that left the ground looking as if it was shrouded in fog. The crowd numbered just 2,500. The proceeds from this game were divided between the Wellington City Council, which controlled the Basin, and the hospital.

It was the visit of the 1888 British side that sparked an interest in rugby in nine-year-old Billy Wallace. He was in Manners Street when a horse-drawn carriage swept past carrying the British rugby team to the Basin. Wallace looked at the tourists, singing on top of the carriage, and thought what a fine life they had.

Billy Wallace went along to the Basin to watch the game, was hooked on rugby and would become one of the finest full-backs to play for the All Blacks.

Wallace (pictured left) went on to play 51 matches for New Zealand, including 11 tests, scoring 382 points, a record at the time. He later became a New Zealand team selector, coach and manager. When he died in 1972, at the age of 93, he was the oldest All Black.

JOSEPH ROMANOS COLLECTION

A road gang begins construction of tracks for horse-drawn trams. This corner, where Ellice Street meets Dufferin Street, like others, posed problems for trams circumnavigating the Basin Reserve. They were the reason why the city council tried, unsuccessfully, to endorse plans that took the tracks through the Basin.

▲ An early example of athletics at the Basin Reserve. During the 1890s, a mile race was contested each year for a silver cup presented by W. Courtenay. The race was dominated by a local draper named Alexander Steven, who won in 1894, 1896 and 1897. Here he is seen pounding towards the finish line, running from north to south along what would today be the front of the Museum Stand. Besides often being used for athletics events, the Basin was frequently the finishing point of harrier races.

▶ A scene that has been repeated for two centuries, in a variety of ways, at cricket grounds all over the world. At least six matches are taking place (some with extremely small boundaries) at the Basin Reserve, watched by a sizeable crowd. Oblivious to the cricket are a group of children, ranging in age from a baby in a pram to some youngsters, more intent on amusing themselves by swinging on the wires attached to the flagpole that used to be found in the north-west corner of the ground.

The Edward Dixon Memorial Clock, one of the enduring sights at the Basin Reserve, is in the centre of the Caledonian Stand. It was named after Edward Dixon, a well-known Wellington businessman with a particular passion for cricket. (In 1877, a cricket match was played at the Basin with both sides made up entirely of Dixon family members.)

Edward Dixon died on 22 October 1890, the date commemorated on the plaque under the clock. His son, Joseph, wrote to the mayor the following year on behalf of the family 'for leave to erect a suitable clock on the Caledonian Grandstand to perpetuate the memory of our father'. Approval was granted and the local firm Messrs Littlejohn was commissioned to make the clock. The clockwork-driven original was put in place in 1892 but disappeared during the demolition of the grandstand in 1923.

A new electric-driven clock, made by Timetec Arnold Wright Ltd, appeared over the main door of the stand that was opened in 1925. The Edward Dixon Memorial Clock is now situated above the entrance to the New Zealand Cricket Museum.

The first great Wellington cricketer was Ernie Upham, a medium-fast bowler who was the Ewen Chatfield of his day. Upham, born in 1872, picked up wickets in prodigious numbers. His accuracy, stamina and perseverance were too much for most batsmen. He had an easy-flowing action and delivered the ball from a good height.

He made his first-class debut for Wellington in 1892. Shortly after, bowling on his favourite Basin Reserve, he had match figures of 9– 85 against Otago. He never looked back, often combining with Frank Ashbolt to form a lethal bowling combination. Upham did not make the most of his batting ability, but did score the first century in Wellington senior club cricket – 102 not out against Phoenix in 1893.

In his final first-class match, against Canterbury in 1910, he took 6 for 52, not bad for a 36-year-old. In 49 first-class games, he took 265 wickets at an average of just 16.65.

Upham was lethal in club cricket, finishing with 783 wickets at 9.77, the lowest average of any bowler to have cracked the magic 500 mark. For two decades, he was a Midland stalwart and spearheaded them to 12 championship titles before moving to Northern late in his club career.

Upham so greatly impressed the famous English umpire Jim Phillips in 1898 that he asked the Wellington man to accompany him to England, where, he assured Upham, he could enter any county side. There was little chance that Upham would accept the offer. He had joined Bell Gully Izard in 1890 and remained with them until his death in 1935.

At the end of the century, enthusiastic crowds paid to watch balloonists give exhibitions in balloons filled with hydrogen gas. After rising into the sky, they would jump from their balloon, making a dramatic descent by parachute. Before they leapt off, they released the gas so that the balloon fluttered to earth to be used for the next performance. Captain Charles Lorraine was one such aeronautical exhibitionist.

Captain Lorraine was the stage name of David Mahoney, who was born in 1872 in Auckland, where he grew up. But he was of a roving disposition and travelled to Australia, and then England, where he took up the profession of ballooning and became an expert aeronaut and parachutist, making a number of successful ascents around such London sites as Earl's Court, Kew Gardens, Alexandra Palace and Crystal Palace. Twice he crossed the English Channel in a balloon.

In 1898, Mahoney returned to New Zealand as Captain Lorraine, 'The King of Parachutists'. He starred at the Auckland Exhibition, and made jumps from the Auckland Domain and Ellerslie Racecourse. Lorraine then journeyed to Wellington, finding time to marry Frances Juriss of Christchurch along the way. In Wellington, on 4 October 1899, he made ascents in the *Empress* balloon from the Basin Reserve.

A huge crowd, some within the Basin, some outside, watched the balloon take off and climb to a height of about 700 metres, but a breeze blew Lorraine a short distance away south-east and he was unable to parachute back into the ground as he had intended. He abandoned his balloon above St Mark's Church and parachuted to safety in the grounds of Wellington College.

Captain Lorraine continued south to Christchurch and made an ascent from Lancaster Park that ended in tragedy. His parachute broke free as the balloon began to rise. Strong winds blew the *Empress* a mile out to sea, where it collapsed, and Lorraine was drowned.

Captain Charles Lorraine, 'King of the Parachutists'

The *Empress* balloon at Lancaster Park, Christchurch, from where it was blown out to sea and collapsed, drowning Lorraine.

Maori carnivals were held at the Basin Reserve and at Lancaster Park in 1900 and 1903. The British Government had rejected New Zealand Prime Minister Richard John Seddon's call for 'our dark-skinned fellow subjects' to serve in the Boer War, feeling political considerations peculiar to South Africa rendered it impossible. The carnivals were staged to show the citizens of Christchurch and Wellington the Maori in their natural environment performing poi dances, haka and ancient waiata sung to the accompaniment of the koauau, or Maori flute. The carnivals were seen as a way to reinforce Maori allegiance to the Crown. In today's terms, it was a public relations exercise.

A haka is performed at the Basin. The 11 bell tents provided overnight accommodation and the two large marquees were for entertaining. This is perhaps the clearest photograph of the site of the Wakefield Memorial. It was common at this time for Wellingtonians to refer to the 'fountain' side of the ground.

Left to right:

The public at the northern end of the Basin awaits the arrival of the band.

The Maori band from Otaki leads the participants into the ground.

A hangi is served in the south-west corner of the Basin.

The star of the New Zealand track and field championships at the Basin Reserve in March 1900 was George Smith, of Auckland, seen here second from left during the 440 yards hurdles. Smith won this event, as well as the 120 yards hurdles, and the 100 and 220 yards sprints. What's more, he won them all in one afternoon, and ran heats in each event just for good measure.

George Smith is arguably the greatest all-round sportsman in New Zealand history. He was born in Auckland in 1874 and, growing up in a racing family, became a stable boy at 14. He later took out a jockey's licence and rode Impulse to win the New Zealand Cup in 1894.

Smith possessed great speed and when he took up rugby he was a sensation as a winger. He represented New Zealand in 1897, 1901 and 1905, appearing in 39 matches and scoring 34 tries. He would have played many more times for New Zealand, but his athletics commitments often ruled him out.

When Bert Baskiville organised a team to play Northern Union (rugby league) in Britain in 1907–08, George Smith was one of the first names he wrote down. Smith, always something of an entrepreneur, became vice-captain of the All Golds, as they were tagged, and did a substantial amount of the recruiting of other players for the trip. Later, he signed to play professionally for Oldham, and his league career stretched through until 1916.

Apart from winning 15 national athletics titles, Smith won three Australasian and one British championships. In 1904, he set an unofficial 440-yard hurdles world record of 58.5 seconds.

Smith's times at the Basin were remarkable. The surface was so uneven that when runners lined up and surveyed the hurdles, they found them angled every which way. In addition, whereas today's hurdlers leap over 3-foot hurdles, those in Smith's day were 3 feet 6 inches. As he was only 5 feet 7 inches tall, Smith was certainly a phenomenal athlete.

ALEXANDER TURNBULL LIBRARY

FOUR

A Time of Growth

1901–1920

J. P. FIRTH, the famous headmaster of Wellington College, used to delight in regaling friends with the story of the time the mayor of Wellington said to him, 'Do you know, Mr Firth, that our engineer tells me it costs the city £2,000 a year in wear and tear around the corners of the Basin Reserve.' Firth replied, 'If that is all it costs to preserve this central ground for the citizens of Wellington, then it is cheap at the price.'

The story says a lot about Firth and the Basin of the early years of the twentieth century. As the long-serving headmaster of a prestigious boys' college, Firth was a significant person in the Wellington community, able to speak frankly with the mayor. He was also an astute thinker and appreciated what the Basin meant to Wellington.

The Basin continued to cause consternation to city council engineers and accountants. Common sense told them it would be far more practical to have the trams running directly from Adelaide Road into Kent and Cambridge Terraces, but there was the small matter of Wellington's major sports ground in the way. Thus much time and trouble, and expense, was required to build and maintain the tracks that bent around the Basin.

The ground was constantly under threat. In 1904, there was an attempt to induce the city council to obtain parliamentary authority to run an electric tram through the Basin. The question was left in abeyance. The matter did go to Parliament in 1915, when the Basin Reserve Bill was proposed upon the recommendation of the Lands Committee, and would have had the Basin traversed with a tramline. The matter was debated for three days, after which the House of Representatives refused the recommendation.

New Zealand underwent enormous change in this period. Two major wars – the Boer War and the First World War – came and went. Queen Victoria's 63-year reign ended in 1901. In 1907, New Zealand was given Dominion status. The population soared. Within the 20 years to 1921, the Wellington Provincial District population nearly doubled, to 248,801. The completion of the Main Trunk line in 1909 made travel from Wellington to other parts of the country far easier.

By 1901, 141,354 people lived in Wellington Provincial District. The citizens used the Basin Reserve for any number of purposes besides sport, ranging from Maori cultural exhibitions, to Dominion Day gatherings, to major fundraising events to coronation celebrations. Whenever a large crowd was expected, the Basin was the natural venue. But it remained principally a sports ground, even if there was little overall direction in the way it was run. For instance, for many years city council staff attended to the eastern side of the ground, and the Wellington Cricket Association paid to have the western side looked after.

Cricket remained the main sport played at the ground. World-famous players like Pelham Warner, Victor Trumper, Clem Hill and Warwick Armstrong played at the Basin. There were local heroes, too, including Ernie Upham, Arnold Williams, Fred Midlane, Stan Brice, Ken Tucker and Wiri Baker. There was, in hindsight, much to lament when a young man named Clarrie Grimmett, who had played nine matches for Wellington before the First World War, emigrated to Australia.

With the introduction of the Plunket Shield in 1906–07, cricket became more organised nationally, but Wellington struggled to produce good practice wickets and there were often complaints about the state of the Basin surface. The reasons for this are not hard to fathom. Except for Karori and Kilbirnie, every club used the Basin as its practice ground, and for some years practices were run on every weekday night.

Of course, the Basin was a much bigger field back

then, and on the eastern side there was the Common, where all the youngsters in the neighbourhood would converge to play pick-up games of cricket or football.

Soccer and women's hockey, which had used the Basin only irregularly, were granted regular access to the ground from 1908, and the first hockey test played in New Zealand took place on 30 September 1914. The New Zealand women's team, 'the All Blacks of hockey', as they were called, played England in front of 4,000 spectators. The Englishwomen won an entertaining match 6–5, having led 3–1 at halftime. Manawatu beat Wellington 3–2 in the curtain-raiser.

Rugby league was first seen at the Basin in 1914, when a British team beat Wellington 14–7. In 1919, the Basin hosted the Australia v. New Zealand test match. At a time when league officials could not find suitable headquarters in Wellington, the Basin gave them a life-line. The following season, New Zealand took on Great Britain at the Basin and went down 10–11.

The national athletics champs were held at the Basin in 1900 and frequently after that. Stars like George Smith, Gerald Keddell and Harry Kerr arrived in town and swept New Zealand titles. The Basin was the home track of Jack Hempton, the first New Zealander to break 10 seconds for the 100 yards.

For Wellingtonians, the Basin was very much all things to all people. Club lacrosse matches were held on Saturdays during winter in the years before the First World War. The teams involved were Capitol, Wellington, Columbia and Kelburn.

The Basin was the place for the ladies to dress in their Sunday best, complete with parasol and large hat, and be seen walking.

In *Old Wellington Days*, Pat Lawlor described the Basin as a sanctuary. 'It was a children's paradise,' he wrote, 'with its many trees, winding paths, quaint enclosures with high fences around them, wooden turnstiles, merry-go-round and sloping grassy banks to roll down. A small boy's ambition was to do five miles of running and walking around the grassy boundary, but they were distracted by the above and the pine trees. The children were delighted when caretaker "Fatty Strong" used Dobbin to pull the heavy roller. He put canvas spats on Dobbin's hooves to protect the grass.'

Coronation Day for King Edward VI in 1902. Note the the loudspeaker attached to a wigwam frame. There appears to be as many spectators outside the Basin Reserve in Buckle Street as there are on the bank.

Charles Twist was the curator of the Basin Reserve for 31 years, until 1913. Huge changes took place in his time, including the building of the curator's new home, in front of which he and his family proudly pose at its opening in 1907. It was built at the top of the bank in the north-west corner and had a vegetable garden that was the envy of many spectators.

ALEXANDER TURNBULL LIBRARY

ALEXANDER TURNBULL LIBRARY

One of the Basin Reserve's oldest neighbours, the Caledonian Hotel, undergoes change. Built in 1875, it became an oasis for sportsmen watching games at the Basin. It was originally a two-storey wooden building with a balcony on the top floor. In 1902, it was reduced in size to enable trams to make an easier turn into Adelaide Road.

▲ Because there were no playing fields in Te Aro, the eastern side of the Basin Reserve from the earliest days was designated a 'Common', where children could play.

▼ 16 January 1903. Lord Hawke's English XI was the sixteenth overseas team to tour New Zealand since 1864. Thirteen had played at the Basin Reserve. Lord Hawke's team played 18 matches in New Zealand, and gave 11 minor associations exposure to some of England's test players, led by Pelham Warner. The Wellington Cricket Association had to pay a guarantee of £250 to stage the match.

Warner wrote *Cricket Across the Seas* after the tour and commented in it: 'The City of Wellington was given a public half-holiday for the match and when the English side took the field, a fine welcome was given them by a crowd of 5,000.

'The Basin Reserve presented a fine sight. The authorities had cause to put up screens to prevent those who could not or would not pay a shilling, from seeing the game, but this hardly had the desired effect, for some tore holes in the screens, others placed bicycles along the fence and stood on the saddles and others climbed over the fence without being noticed. Everyone seemed for the time to have gone cricket-mad.'

More than 16,000 spectators paid at the gate during the three days, making it the best-attended match in Wellington to that time.

▲ Postcards printed in Germany of scenic spots in New Zealand were all the rage in the early twentieth century. One of many that appeared is of Jupp's Band giving a Sunday afternoon concert from the bandstand at the Basin Reserve.

New Zealand's greatest gift to Australian cricket, Clarrie Grimmett, lived in Roxburgh Street, near the Embassy Theatre. Three boys of the Harris family lived next door. When they were aged 15, 10 and 8, and young Clarrie was 6, he was entrusted to carry the spade that they used to flatten out the area on the Common where they pitched their wickets. As all three Harris boys bowled leg-spinners, it is not surprising that Clarrie followed suit.

Grimmett played for Wellington, but after being a non-travelling reserve for the New Zealand team that toured Australia in 1913–14, he emigrated to Australia at the age of 26. When he was 34, his perseverance was rewarded when he was chosen to play for Australia against England in 1925 and claimed 5–45 and 6–37. He was the first bowler to take 200 wickets in test cricket, eventually capturing 216 wickets in 37 matches.

Grimmett was a small, gnome-like cricketer who always bowled in his cap, hiding a balding forehead. He took a short, springy run-up and bowled with a bustling, almost round-arm action. His trajectory was low and his length remarkable.

◄ During summer evenings, residents from the houses overlooking the Basin Reserve on the slopes of Mount Victoria would wander down to the ground to watch clubs practise.

It is interesting to note that transport was by way of bicycles (foreground) or tramcars, in this case a double-decker (background). On the eastern side of the ground, children played their games on the Common.

▼ New Zealand played the Australian cricket team that was en route to England at the Basin on 16 March 1905. A crowd of more than 10,000 packed the ground on the first day. Clarrie Grimmett, aged 14, tore a hole in his new blue suit jumping the barbed wire on the top of the fence surrounding the ground. He saw Victor Trumper and Clem Hill add 269 for the fifth wicket in 117 minutes. Grimmett maintained that Trumper's 172 was the finest innings he ever saw.

This view from the tower of St Patrick's College shows the wear marks on the Common and the practice areas at the north and south ends.

N.Z.A.A.A. CHAMPIONSHIP MEETING
(H.E.KERR (WGTON) WINNING THE ONE MILE: 6"46."
ZAK PHOTO: 1.2.08:   539.

The first New Zealander to win an Olympic medal was Harry Kerr, of Taranaki, who on 14 July 1908 took the bronze medal in the 3,500 metres walk at the London Olympics, representing Australasia.

For some years Kerr had competed as a professional walker. He applied for amateur status in 1905 and, after a two-year stand-down period, soon made his mark at national level.

Above, he is seen winning the one-mile event at the New Zealand championships at the Basin Reserve in 1908. His victory earned him Olympic selection and set him on the way to holding a unique position in New Zealand sports history.

The caption to this photograph fails to mention that this was a walking race, which makes Kerr's time for the mile seem rather slow.

After the Olympics, Kerr dominated the national scene. His greatest walk was at the national champs in Wellington in 1911 when he won the three-mile race in 21 minutes 36.6 seconds, which remained the national record until 1946. He retired in 1913, but when the national champs were held in nearby Wanganui in 1925, Kerr, aged 46, decided to make a comeback.

He shocked by scooping the one- and three-mile titles. The *New Zealand Herald* headlined its report 'Wonderful Performance For Man Of His Age' and described his feat as 'little short of marvellous'.

Javelin thrower Stan Lay, recalling the championship 70 years later, said. 'I was just a boy then, and it was my first big meet. Like everyone, I was amazed by Harry Kerr. He was a big name because he had won an Olympic medal, and had a good following. To come back and win both titles made him the talk of the championships.'

Harry Kerr died in 1951.

▲ On 19 April 1906, San Francisco was shaken to its foundations by a disastrous earthquake. At least 500 of the regions's inhabitants were killed and 250,000 left homeless. Devastating fires caused by broken gas mains raged out of control. Within a fortnight, a pageant, featuring the police and armed services, was held at the Basin Reserve was held to assist with the San Francisco Earthquake Fund.

▶ Proud medallists from a handicap distance race during the Combined Banks sports day at the Basin Reserve in 1907. The race was won by Renai (Bank of New Zealand) on the right, who was off 10 yards. Second went to Harry Robertson (Bank of New South Wales), centre, who was off scratch. Picot (BNZ) on the left, was off 64 yards and finished third. The three athletes are facing where the R. A. Vance Stand is these days.

55

HOSPITAL SUNDAY
WELLINGTON: N.Z. 13·12·08
"ZAK" PHOTO: 2922.

▶ Many schools and colleges used the Basin Reserve for their school sports. On 12 November 1908, Wellington photographer 'Zak' captured some of the staff at the St Patrick's College sports day. From left: Father B. J. Gondringer, Dean P. J. Smith, Dean P. Regnault, Father J. Ainsworth and Father T. Gilbert. Results and house points were kept on the blackboard on the easel in front of the Caledonian Grandstand.

◀ Nurses in their crisp white uniforms and head-dresses pose behind the grandstand with a collection blanket on 'Hospital Sunday', 13 December 1908.

▲ Players from the Midland Cricket Club stand with spectators for a club game on 17 November 1908. The groundsman's shed is in the middle of the southern end.

The player with the pads on is Arnold Williams. When he played for Canterbury in 1886 as a 17-year-old, he batted two and a half hours for nine runs and earned a reputation as 'the Prince of Stonewallers'. He was selected for New Zealand as a wicketkeeper-batsman in 1896–97.

Williams transferred to Wellington and in his first innings, against Canterbury, he made 163. Little was heard of him for several years. However, in 1907 he scored a polished 100 for Wellington against the touring MCC team and was named as captain of New Zealand for the second international, to be played at the Basin Reserve in March 1907. His outstanding 72 not out in the second innings helped his team win by 56 runs, to give New Zealand their first victory over an English team.

New Zealand's designation as a colony disappeared on 25 November 1907, and was replaced by the official title 'Dominion of New Zealand'. One year later, Dominion Day celebrations were held at the Basin Reserve (right). Sir Joseph Ward and other dignitaries addressed the huge crowd that fanned out across the field, though they did not have use of a loudspeaker system, or even a megaphone. The press, in front of the dais to the left, are faithfully recording the Prime Minister's every word. In the background of the crowd scene above is the white scoreboard, the first permanent cricket scoreboard installed at the ground.

An athletics meeting prior to the First World War. Solidly built hurdles dominate the centre of the ground, while the public's attention is centred on the pole vault taking place in front of the grandstand. It is highly likely that the competition included Len McKay of Wellington, who won five national pole vault championships from 1907 to 1913. He also won New Zealand long jump, triple jump and shot put titles.

A women's 100 yards race in one of the popular athletics meetings at the Basin Reserve.
Note the lanes are marked with raised rope. The Caledonian Hotel has a grandstand view.

Members of different branches of the armed forces enjoyed congregating at the Basin
Reserve and displaying their marching skills, often accompanied by brass-band music.

61

England v. Wellington: Snapshots at the Ladies' Hockey Contest.

Stan Brice (right) was one of the great identities of Wellington sport through the first four decades of the twentieth century, and, because of his tremendous hitting, a particular crowd favourite at the Basin Reserve.

'Sixer' Brice, as he was known, played senior club cricket for 33 years, enjoyed outstanding success for Wellington, mainly as a pace bowler, and captained New Zealand. He also made his name in rugby, as a wing forward for Petone and Wellington.

Although he was nearly 33 years old when the First World War began, his cricket improved with age. He took 9–67 against Auckland at the Basin in 1919 and used his height to get the ball to bounce disconcertingly. When Vernon Ransford's Australians arrived in New Zealand in 1921, Brice, 41, led New Zealand in the two 'tests'. In the first, at the Basin, he had match figures of 7–80.

He was at the centre of a selection wrangle when Archie MacLaren brought an MCC team to New Zealand in 1923. After taking three wickets and scoring usefully in the first 'test', he was dropped for the second. But he bowled beautifully for Wellington against the tourists on a helpful Basin pitch, and took 5–52 and 5–45. The New Zealand team, which had been agreed upon but not named, was then released without Brice, which caused an uproar. The captain, Nessie Snedden, quit in protest and Brice replaced him in what would be his last appearance for New Zealand.

Brice and his good mate Herb McGirr were an inseparable pair. When Wellington played Otago in 1925, Brice was dismissed by Otago fast bowler George Dickinson when he mistimed a hook. The ball came off the edge of his bat, hit him on the head and Dickinson caught the rebound. Brice recovered consciousness in the pavilion and caused mirth when he said: 'I thought I was in heaven, for I found a parson [Blamires, the former Wellingtonian, then represent-

DON NEELY COLLECTION

ing Otago], bending over me. Then I saw McGirr and knew I wasn't.'

Brice played club cricket until 1935, for Phoenix, Hutt and Petone. His 8,349 runs places him near the top of the all-time club batting lists, but no-one even approaches him as a bowler, his 1,173 wickets being 300 more than the next best.

He was a provincial selector and, from 1925 to 1932, a national selector. He became known as the 'Grand Old Man' of Wellington cricket, and was always popular. Brice kept busy in winter, too. After his rugby days were over, he turned to rugby league, helping to introduce the game in the capital.

◀ In 1914, an England women's hockey team toured New Zealand, delighting locals with their skill. They played the first hockey test ever in New Zealand, on Wednesday, 30 September 1914, winning 6–5. Eight weeks earlier, the Englishwomen had attracted a crowd of 5,500 to the Basin Reserve when beating Wellington 8–0. The *New Zealand Freelance* devoted a full page to the match.

▶ When Great Britain declared war on Germany on 4 August 1914, New Zealand's reaction was immediate. Early in 1915, troops march along Rugby Street past the groundsman's cottage on the left and the Caledonian Hotel on the right. St Mark's Church towers over proceedings. The tram tracks that caused so much discussion bend into Adelaide Road.

ALEXANDER TURNBULL LIBRARY

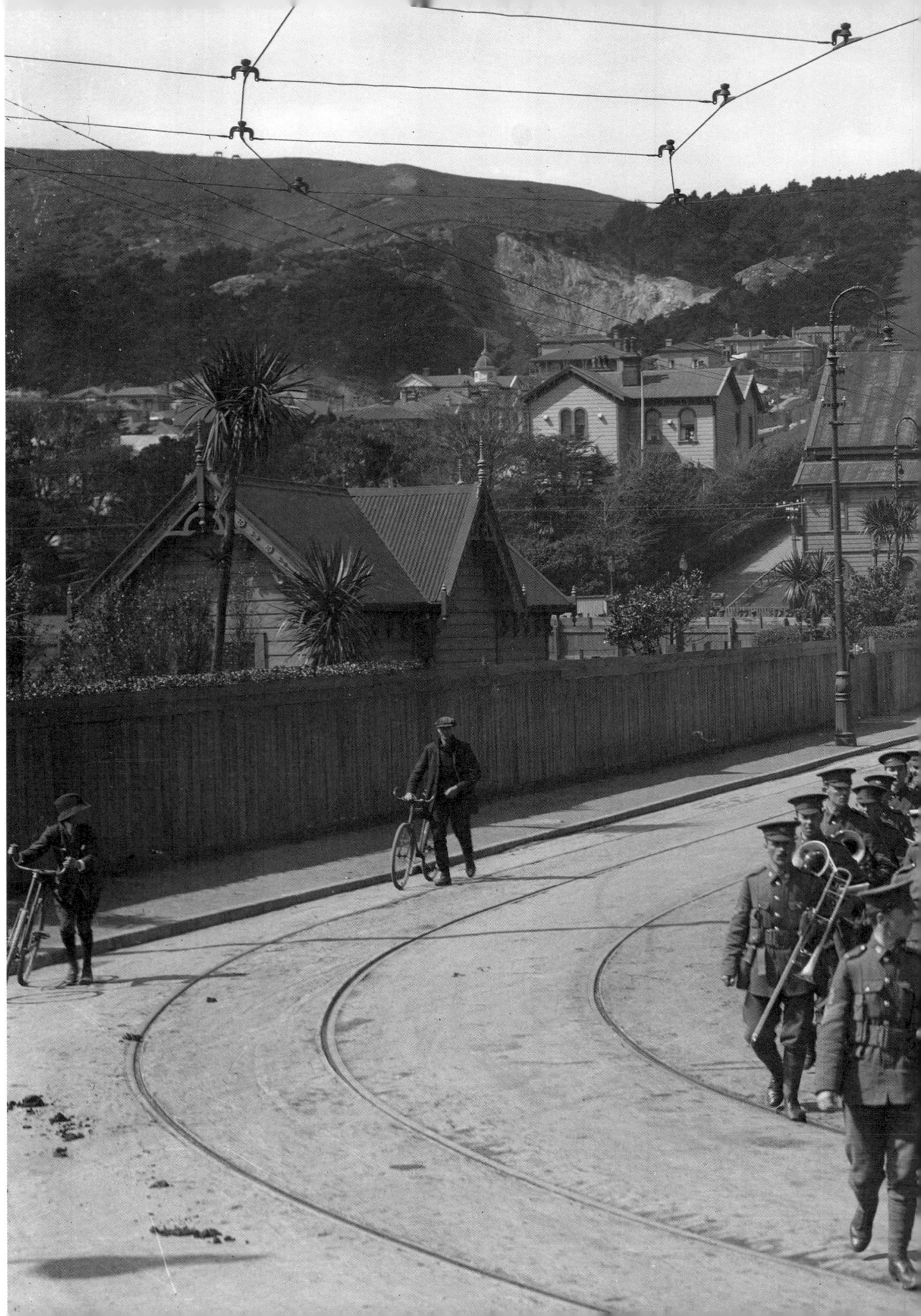

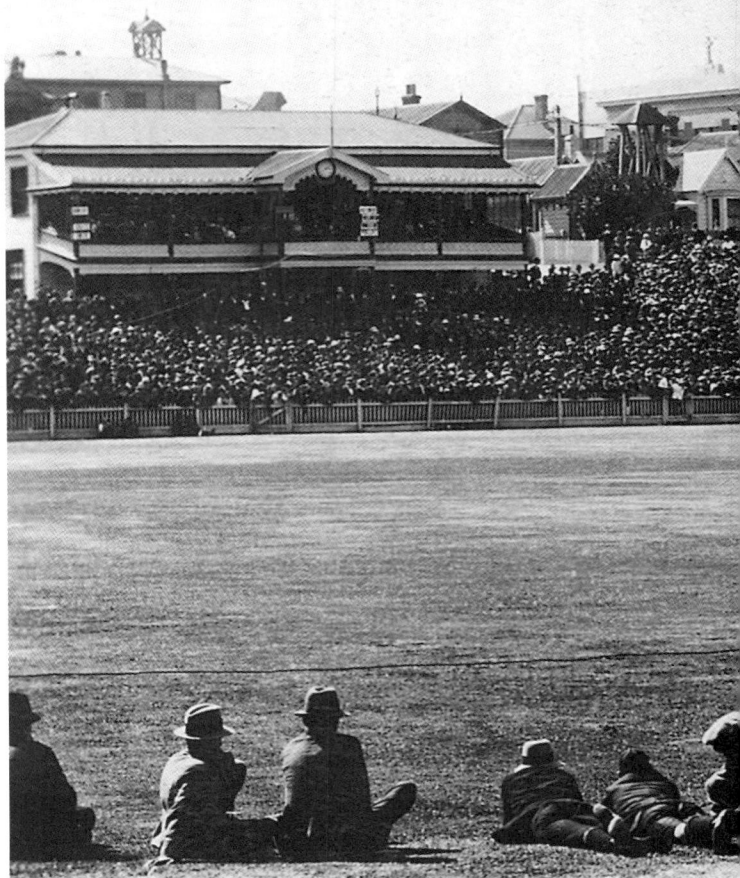

▶ A notable game of cricket was played at the Basin Reserve over the New Year in 1915. Before a packed bank, Fred Midlane amassed 222 not out, setting a record score for a New Zealander in first-class cricket.

Midlane was an extremely talented batsman who played his first first-class game for Wellington aged 15. Before his twentieth birthday he scored 149 against Otago and 102 against Auckland.

He went to Sydney in an attempt to play for Australia and returned to Wellington six years later. In 1917 he transferred to Auckland.

Midlane holds a unique position, having been involved in a record partnership for Wellington against Auckland, and for Auckland against Wellington.

DON NEELY COLLECTION

▼ In an ironic touch, considering what was to happen, Clarrie Grimmett played his last game for Wellington against Arthur Sims' Australian XI, beginning on 13 February 1914. He departed for Sydney three months later. Note that the scoreboard (right) is now black. The large marquee on the east side probably housed the press.

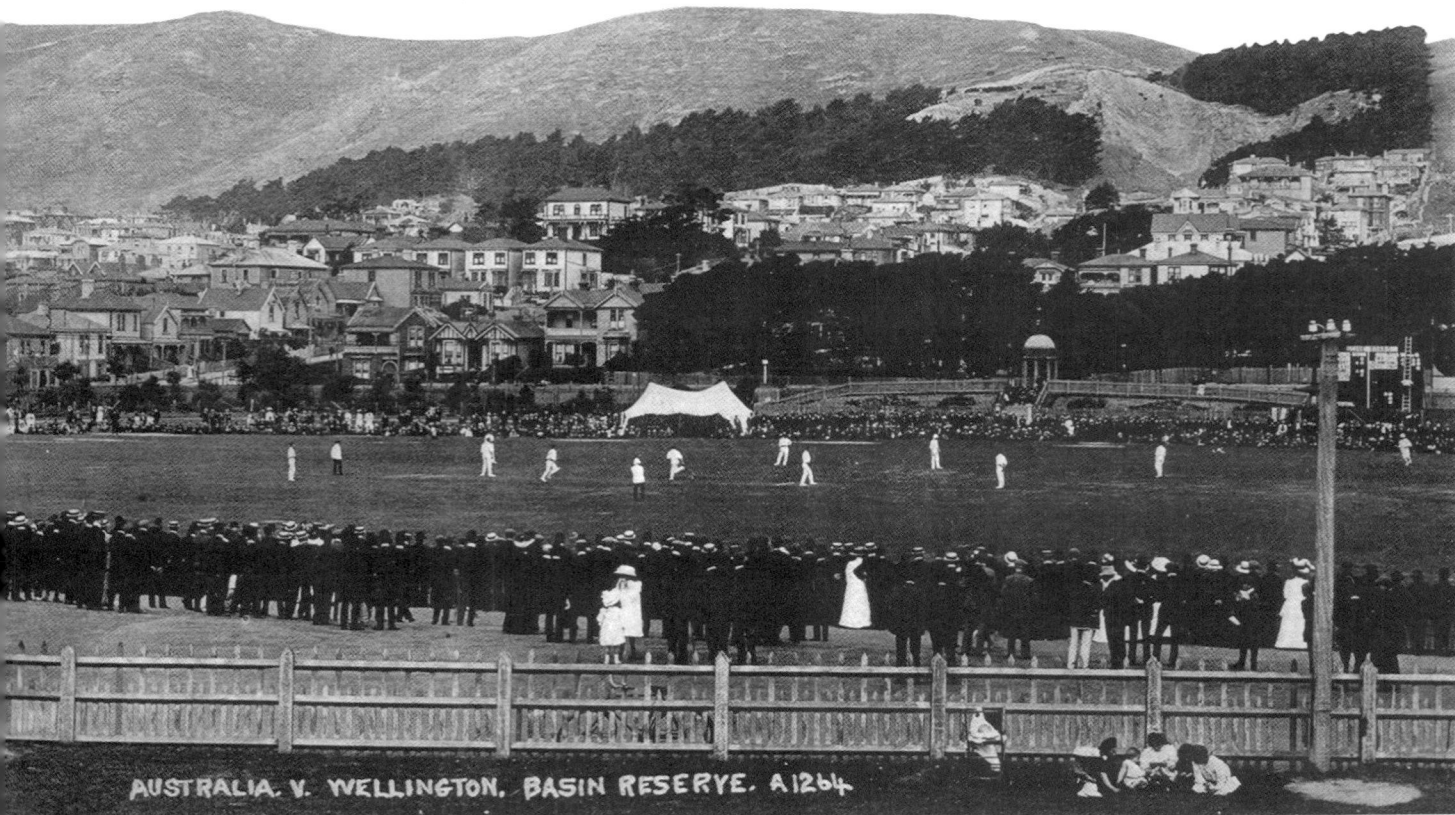

AUSTRALIA. V. WELLINGTON. BASIN RESERVE. A 1264.

NEW ZEALAND CRICKET MUSEUM

Attending a fundraising cricket match in aid of the war effort, Wellington celebrities of 1915 dress in the manner of gentlemen cricketers of 1850.

Photographed with the team is (on left) William Massey, the Prime Minister. Two dignitaries visiting New Zealand at that time, the Earl and Countess of Liverpool, are standing in the centre of the photo. Sir Joseph Ward, former Prime Minister who took the Liberals into William Massey's wartime government, is in playing gear to the right of the visitors.

THE KANGAROO DEFEATS THE MOA AT RUGBY LEAGUE FOOTBALL by 44 to 21

THE NEW ZEALAND TEAM – Murphy (line umpire), A. Morris, G. Iles, S. Walters, J. Scott, W. King, C. Dufty, G. Bradley, H. Avery, S. Lowrie, W Wilson, W Williams, H. Neal, K. Ifwersen (captain), F. Evans (line umpire), A. House (referee).

The Basin Reserve became the country's second rugby league test venue when, on 27 August 1919, New Zealand met a strong Australian team. The New Zealand team was captained by the dynamic Karl Ifwersen, who soon after became one of few players in the pre-professional age permitted to switch from rugby league to rugby union, at which he represented New Zealand against South Africa in 1921. In the above photo of the New Zealand side before the test match, Ifwersen is about to lead them in a haka. He went on to play outstandingly, scoring three tries, but couldn't prevent the visitors winning 44–21. The Kangaroo star was Harold Horder, who is still regarded as one of the greatest players to have represented Australia.

The headline writer for the *New Zealand Freelance* called the New Zealand team the Moa, a tag that did not catch on, though it cropped up occasionally before the Second World War. Rugby league officials were emphatic they wanted the team called the professional All Blacks, and would get annoyed if newspapers resorted to frivolous names. In 1921, an *Auckland Star* writer called the league team the Kiwis and the New Zealand Rugby League protested strongly to the newspaper. Not surprisingly, rugby union officials were eager to preserve the term All Blacks for their game. The situation was resolved in 1938 when the New Zealand Rugby League officially adopted the title of the Kiwis for its national team.

Martin Luckie was one of the enduring figures in Wellington cricket for several decades and was almost a fixture at the Basin Reserve for the first half of the twentieth century. Bowling tantalising left-arm spinners, he made his senior club debut in 1891 and enjoyed such immediate success that he was pulled into the representative team the same season.

Luckie took more than 300 wickets at senior level. But it is for his work as a cricket administrator that he is remembered. Luckie was a key figure in the administration of the Wellington club and also served for an extended period on the Wellington Cricket Association's management committee. He was president of the association from 1936 to 1946 and was later made a life member.

During most cricket matches of the period, first-class and club, Luckie was usually to be found at the Basin Reserve, often wearing his trademark cloth cap.

To honour his contribution to Wellington, which he also served as a city councillor, the large park opposite what is now the Mount Albert hockey centre was officially named Martin Luckie Park.

Among the many sports to make occasional appearances at the Basin Reserve was baseball. As can be seen in this photo, taken in 1920, the sport was treated seriously – note the gear and the scoreboard. Two of the players are wearing cricket boots. Belfast Street, off Rugby Street, is behind the players.

FIVE

A New Grandstand

1921–1940

By the early 1920s, the Caledonian Grandstand, quaint as it was in its prime 60 years earlier, had run its race and it was felt that the Basin Reserve deserved a splendid new stand. In 1923, entries were called for a competition to design a new pavilion. Architect P. H. Graham won the £100 prize, but his design was not used. Instead the City Engineer's department designed a new stand. The contractors were Higgins and Arcus Brothers and work began late in 1924. The new reinforced concrete building was opened a year later, at a cost of £16,710.

It was the replacement of the Caledonian Grandstand that held the greatest significance for the Basin in the period between the wars. Once the decision was made by the city council to invest in a new stand, arguments about the future of the Basin ceased, at least for the time being.

Between the two world wars, there were some momen-

tous occasions at the Basin, few bigger in terms of crowd numbers than the visit of Lord Baden-Powell, founder of the Boy Scouts and Girl Guides, in 1931. Archbishop Redwood's Diamond Jubilee in 1934 seemed to involve the entire city, and celebrations went on for days, with the turnout for the mass at the Basin amazing. There were the usual Anzac Day parades, band contests and the like, but the Basin remained primarily a sports ground.

Groundsman Budge Brewer complained to the Wellington Cricket Association that the park was being overused. Monday evening practices were cut out, which gave him slightly more time to prepare the ground. But the situation did not improve enough, so Friday practices

Boy Scouts, Girl Guides, Cubs, Brownies and Sea Scouts turned out in their thousands to meet their founder, Lord Baden-Powell, in 1931.

NEW ZEALAND CRICKET MUSEUM

were dropped as well. At that time it was customary to play two junior games and two senior games on the Basin each weekend.

Brewer was remembered by Governor-General Sir Denis Blundell (1972–77) with affection from his time playing at the Basin in the 1920s and 1930s. Brewer was always extremely popular. It was he who presented Frank Mooney with a bat for making his famous 180 for Wellington against Auckland in 1943.

Overseas cricket teams played at the Basin most seasons, and a succession of fine players turned up. Archie MacLaren, Charlie Macartney, Clarrie Grimmett, Bill Ponsford, Frank Woolley, Herbert Sutcliffe and Walter Hammond were among dozens of great cricketers who played there between the wars.

In 1928, an Australian XI led by Vic Richardson beat Wellington by four wickets. Ponsford, Bill Woodfull, Alan Kippax, Richardson himself, wicketkeeper Bert Oldfield and off-spinner Don Blackie all showed their ability, but the man who attracted most attention was little leg-spinner Clarrie Grimmett, who made the match a happy home-coming by taking 3–65 and 4–94 to help bowl the tourists to victory.

Another big game was in 1935 when Wellington beat Errol Holmes' MCC team by 14 runs.

The most significant match was the test against England in 1930, when Stewie Dempster and Jack Mills scored centuries, Mills on debut. This was only New Zealand's second test. One of the most interested spectators was a Christchurch 14-year-old named Walter Hadlee, later to become one of New Zealand's best batsmen, a test captain and a long-serving national administrator. In 1930, he parked himself under the scoreboard on the eastern side of the ground and kept the score meticulously, showing neatness and attention to detail that would later serve him well as an accountant. With the official scorebook long since misplaced, Hadlee's scorekeeping takes on extra significance.

There were all sorts of high-quality athletics at the Basin, and not just the national championships that were allocated to Wellington frequently, but also Canterbury v. Wellington rep fixtures, the provincial championships and special meetings to take advantage of visits of overseas athletes. The most famous race was American Leo Lermond's victory by inches over Randlolph Rose over a mile in 1930.

There were many champions to be seen at the Basin at this time, including throwers Peter Munro and Jack McHolm and hurdler Harry Wilson. Sprinters Norma Wilson, Elaine Martin, of Christchurch, and Thelma Kench, of Wanganui, broke records on the Basin, but their times were not recognised internationally. The Basin, with its strong winds and uneven surface, did not meet record-setting requirements. Another sprinter, Doreen Lumley, ran impressively at the Basin in 1938 and looked a superstar in the making. She became the first New Zealander to set an official world record, but tragically she and her twin sister were killed shortly after in a road crash. Just before the war, both Pat Boot, in the 880 yards and mile, and Ces Matthews, over longer distances, ran so well on the Basin that they hinted at what might have been if the 1940 Olympics had not been cancelled.

Jack Mills (left) and Stewie Dempster walk on to the Basin Reserve at the start of the first test to be played there, in 1930. Note that Mills, a left-hander, has only one batting glove. Both batsmen scored centuries, and their partnership of 276, meticulously recorded in Walter Hadlee's scorebook (below), remains a record against England.

ALL CRICKETERS SHOULD POSSESS THE BUSSEY **DIARY AND COMPANION. PRICES 6d and 1/-**
PACKED WITH CRICKET INFORMATION AND RECORDS EXTENDING OVER 48 YEARS.

Umpires A. Cave & L. Coleroft

MATCH BETWEEN New Zealand **and** M.C.C. (English Team)

1st **INNINGS** N.Z. **PLAYED AT** Basin Reserve (Wellington) **DATE** Jan. 24th 1930

Mins at crease		Batsman.	Score.	How Out.	Bowlers.	Total.	Chance
240	11.30 1 5.15	C.S. Dempster		std Cornford	Woolley	136	3
253	11.30 2 4.58	J.E. Mills		bowled	Woolley	117	3
22	5.10 3 6.12	T.C. Lowry		ct Duleepsinhji	Woolley	6	
104	5.16 4 12.29	M.L. Page		ct Cornford	Allom	67	
77	5.24 5 12.9	R.C. Blunt		ct Duleepsinhji	Woolley	36	
38	12.10 6 12.48	C.A. McLeod		bowled	Woolley	16	
3	12.31 7 12.34	G.L. Weir		l.b.w.	Woolley	3	
21	12.36 8 12.57	K.C. James		ct Cornford	Worthington	7	
14	12.50 9 1.4	G.R. Dickinson		ct Worthington	Woolley	5	
1	12.50 10 1.1	W.E. Merritt		l.b.w.	Worthington	0	
3*	1.1 11 1.4	F.T. Badcock		not out		4	
		Byes				14	
		Leg Byes				18	
		Wide Balls					
		No Balls				8	

Rose's popularity did so much for Wellington athletics that it led to the introduction of night athletics.

At the Basin Reserve's 'electric light' meetings of the 1930s, Wellingtonian Alex Hill was a big attraction. Hill became an expert in the sack race, so much so that he even set world records over 75 and 100 yards on 12 February 1938. Hill, a prominent competitive walker who won the national one-mile title in 1930, was amazingly proficient at sack racing and generated surprising speed, despite strict rules dictating where the sack had to be tied. Athletes would put one foot in each of two corners. When Hill competed, the world's best time for 75 yards was 10.8 seconds, set by R. Mercer, of Rochester, USA, in 1904. Hill covered the journey in 10.1 seconds. J. Finn, of Brooklyn, New York, had held the 100 yards record of 14.2 seconds since 1929. Hill lowered it to 13.6 seconds, and then 13.4. Many athletes would be quite happy to

match this even without the sack! Hill generally competed without opposition.

The electric light meetings were full of entertainment. Besides the regular athletics events and Hill's sack expertise, Alf Jenkins and his troupe would entertain the crowd with acrobatics exhibitions, and there would be a variety of musical performances.

Hockey – both men's and women's – was played at the Basin intermittently. Until the Mount Albert Stadium was built in the early 1980s, Wellington struggled for a good hockey venue. While the Basin's undulating surface was not ideal, it was as good as most parks and the ground offered sizeable crowd capacity.

Several Australian men's teams toured between the two world wars. On 8 August 1925, New Zealand beat the Australians 5–1 at the Basin, with Eric Watts making the occasion more remarkable by becoming the first

Women's soccer on the Basin Reserve in September 1921. Before the Auckland v. Wellington Brown Shield match, two women's teams, Aotea A and Aotea B, played a curtain-raiser that proved exceedingly popular with the spectators. The players were drawn from a factory that made men's shirts.

In 1926, a King's Birthday crowd of 15,000 – a staggering number, considering a full house today at a one-day cricket international is 13,000 – watched the Indian Army hockey team beat Wellington 8–3, having led 5–1 at halftime. The star of the show was the incomparable Dhyan Chand, who scored five of the Indians' goals and introduced spectators to a level of hockey not previously seen in New Zealand.

New Zealand player to score a hat-trick of goals in a test. Wellington beat Australia several times in this period. In 1922, the home side won 4–3 at the Basin, in 1929 it was 7–2, and in 1934 the score was 3–1.

New Zealand hosted a number of Indian men's hockey teams, and they usually stopped off at the Basin. An Indian Army side toured in 1926 and proved very popular. The first Indian side to play a test at the Basin was in 1935, when Dhyan Chand's team beat New Zealand 3–2. In 1938, an Indian team sponsored by the Prince of Manavader toured New Zealand, winning all three test matches. The test at the Basin, played on 30 July, was won 4–0 by the Indians.

English sides tended to be the New Zealand women's main opponents. One much-awaited women's international took place on 21 July 1938, when England, captained by the brilliant defender M. Knott, beat New Zealand in the last match of its tour, 8–2, to complete an unbeaten tour. The England team's uniform, to quote from the match programme, comprised cardinal red tunic and girdle, white blouse and red stockings. This team is still described as one of the best women's hockey sides in history. The curtain-raiser featured a women's match billed as Wellington v. Maoris.

Another big day for women's hockey was 8 August 1936, when New Zealand beat Fiji 4–0. A fortnight earlier, Wellington had beaten Fiji 4–0, also at the Basin. The Fijians caused a stir by playing in shorts.

In the 1920s, soccer established itself at the Basin, which became known as New Zealand's Wembley.

The feature soccer match of the season was the Chatham Cup final. The trophy was presented to New Zealand from the officers and men of HMS *Chatham* on 14 December 1922. The first Chatham Cup – run on FA Cup lines – was held the following year. The first two finals were played at Athletic Park, the third at Newtown Park. In 1926, the final was moved to the Basin, where it stayed until the 1970s.

One early final that was warmly recalled, especially by locals, took place in 1932, when Marist, of Wellington, beat the Millerton All Blacks, of Buller. Future radio broadcaster Peter Sellers, just a youngster then, was taken to the game by his father. There he saw a crowd of 5,000 Wellingtonians cheer on their favourites. 'Millerton played in black. That's where they got the name from,' says Sellers. 'Jim Kershaw, who was later the NZFA chairman, scored a goal for Marist. The weather was great and Marist played exceptionally well.'

There were also international soccer matches to whet the appetite. The first test was in 1924 when New Zealand and Chinese Universities drew 2–2. Cricket star Ces Dacre and Lew Daniels scored for New Zealand. In 1927, New Zealand scored their first win on the Basin, 1–0 over Canada. There was a horrific day for local fans on 11 July 1936, when Australia hammered New Zealand 10–0.

The following year, an English amateur team beat Wellington-Manawatu Combined 6–0 at the Basin. Their star was Bernard Joy, of Arsenal. Though he was an amateur (and never turned professional), he had earned himself a place in history by winning a full cap for England, against Belgium the year before.

There was an unusual occurrence in 1938. Wellington were to play Athletic in the club rugby match at Athletic Park and, on the same afternoon, Wellington were taking on Auckland in a representative soccer fixture at the Basin. Athletic Park was sodden, so rugby was postponed. The soccer was played, and thousands trooped down to the Basin. Perhaps buoyed by the unexpected support, Wellington won 5–4.

The *New Zealand Freelance* covers in photographs the Caledonian sports day in January 1922. Among those pictured are hurdler Harry Wilson, who was fourth in the 1920 Olympic Games 110 metres hurdles final; and Peter Munro, who won a record 29 national men's titles in the shot put, discus and javelin.

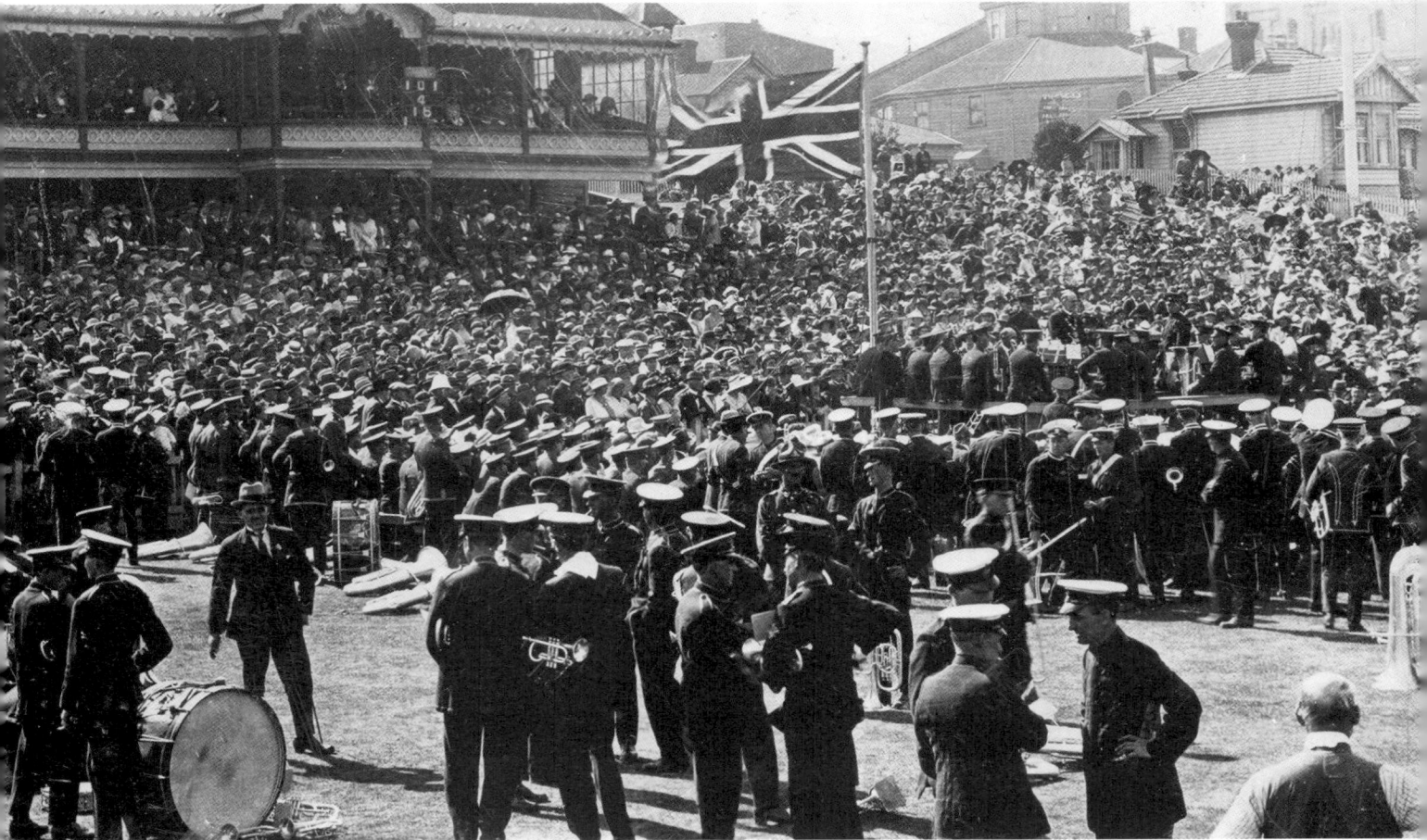

▲ Not much room to spare here. It's 13 February 1922, the opening day of a band contest that has drawn wide interest from competitors and spectators.

▶ A group of dignitaries walks onto the Basin Reserve to inspect the bands. From left: Sir John Luke, the former mayor of Wellington; J. S. Elliott; Lord Jellicoe, Governor-General; and J. P. Firth, former headmaster of Wellington College.

Walking sticks were very much in fashion. Firth had a hollow walking stick that he used to fill with salt. When he walked across the fields at Wellington College or the Basin, he would release some salt onto broad-leaved weeds, thus killing them.

The cricket scoreboard at the Basin Reserve has been located in several parts of the ground. Since 1980, it has occupied its current position, at the southern end. Previously it was to be found for several decades on the eastern side of the ground. In 1923, a scoreboard was built at the northern end, alongside where the C. S. Dempster Gate is today.

▲ Willing hands finish the construction.

▼ The same workers, dressed in suits, sit in front of the finished scoreboard.

Archie MacLaren was aged 51 when he led an MCC team through New Zealand in 1922–23. Two of the three New Zealand v. MCC internationals were played at the Basin, and in the first of them MacLaren defied the sands of time to score an unbeaten 200 in 264 minutes to steer his team to victory by an innings and 156 runs. He damaged his knee and took no further part in the tour. It was the last of his 703 first-class innings.

PARTNERS IN THE THREE-LEGGED RACE

A MERRY SCRAMBLE AT THE NET IN THE OBSTACLE RACE

IN PURSUIT OF THE GREASY PIG

LINED UP FOR THE SACK RACE

**FURTHER INCIDENTS OF THE SPECTACULAR OBSTACLE RACE
THAT WAS KEENLY CONTESTED**

WEEKLY NEWS, ALEXANDER TURNBULL LIBRARY

In 1923, the Royal Navy made a tour of New Zealand with a Special Service Squadron, led by the battlecruiser HMS *Hood*. While in Wellington, the Englishmen took part in an athletics contest at the Basin Reserve.

Competition was not restricted to the more traditional running races, and jumping and throwing competitions, but included events like the egg-and-spoon, three-legged, sack and wheelbarrow races, all usually contested over 100 yards.

WEEKLY NEWS, ALEXANDER TURNBULL LIBRARY

▲ Soccer was the main winter sport at the Basin Reserve for most of the twentieth century. However, for big occasions, rugby league was played there as well because league officials struggled to find a ground of the necessary size elsewhere in Wellington once rugby union had reclaimed Athletic Park.

In August 1924, England played New Zealand in the second test of their tour. The visitors led 11–0 at halftime, but New Zealand fought back bravely to win 13–11. This was the last league test played at the Basin before the Second World War.

▼ Anzac Day processions were once massive affairs, as can be seen by this turnout in 1929. Here marchers gather inside the Basin Reserve before commencing their journey to the Cenotaph.

ALEXANDER TURNBULL LIBRARY

American middle-distance runner Leo Lermond (left) edges out Randolph Rose at an athletics meeting at the Basin Reserve in 1930.

Through the 1920s and early 1930s, Randolph Arthur John Scott Rose, a large and sturdy farmer from the Wairarapa, reached folk-hero status among Wellington sports followers. Rose, a middle-distance runner, took part in a succession of major international races in Wellington against quality opposition such as Americans Lloyd Hahn and Leo Lermond, and always drew many thousands of spectators.

His first appearance on the Basin Reserve was in 1922 at a handicap meeting. He entered the mile and was miffed to find he had been accorded a handicap. Meeting organisers wouldn't listen to his objections, so Rose, given a head start, duly ran away with the race, and made a form of protest by vaulting the finishing tape, which gained him disqualification but met with loud approval from the spectators.

Rose had some famous battles at national championships at the Basin, meeting, and often beating, Auckland distance star Billy Savidan in some epic races.

His last big race on the Basin took place in 1930, when he lined up against American Leo Lermond, who had finished fourth in the 5,000 metres at the previous Olympics. They had a rare old battle, which had the 10,000 spectators screaming with excitement. Finally the American lunged at the tape and won by inches.

Rose's appeal galvanised interest in athletics. Soon any athletics meet, even those not featuring Rose, could be guaranteed a crowd of several thousand. Local officials, capitalising on the sport's popularity, decided to hold what became termed 'electric light meetings'. These were club meetings held at the Basin on Saturday evenings through the early part of the New Year, and took place under lights. This was not the floodlighting we see today, but weak lights strung up by wire, rather like Christmas lights.

These electric light meetings proved a big hit and it became fashionable to be seen in attendance. In 1927, J. G. MacKenzie, the Wellington City Council's director of parks and reserves, reported to the town clerk that the 10 meetings had brought in gate takings of £2,157, of which £807 went to the council and £1,275 to the Wellington Amateur Athletic Association.

The profits from these meetings went towards the building of permanent floodlights at the Basin. These enabled other sports, including soccer, boxing and softball, to be played in the evenings. Historians point to the immense popularity of Rose as a major factor in making these developments possible.

Norma Wilson, originally from Poverty Bay, was one of the big names in the early days of New Zealand women's athletics. She was a world-class sprinter who competed at the 1928 Amsterdam Olympics, the first at which women were permitted to run. Wilson ran many times on the Basin Reserve, and seemed relatively unaffected by the bumpy surface. She ran 11.4 seconds for the 100 yards during the 1927–28 season, and only excessive wind assistance prevented her time being recognised as a New Zealand record.

Wilson retired after the Amsterdam Games, and was married briefly to New Zealand's Olympic gold-medallist boxer Ted Morgan. In 1933, she returned to the track and, in what athletics historian Peter Heidenstrom regards as one of the finest displays ever by a New Zealand sprinter, won the national title in a time of 11 seconds. All four stop watches agreed on the time, but the fact that there was a drop in the Basin track from start to finish prevented a world record being ratified.

Wilson was a brilliant natural athlete and something of a rebel. On her return from the 1928 Olympics, she attended a Government reception and called

on 'those stuffed shirts in Wellington' to put down cinder tracks.

Her actions also led to women wearing shorts instead of the costumes that were the fashion at the time. She was invited to run at an international meet at the Basin and wired Wellington officials, saying: 'No shorts, no show.' Wilson got her way.

Not everyone who has appeared at the Basin Reserve has been a top athlete. For many years, Wellesley College, then situated on The Terrace in Wellington, and today at Days Bay, brought their children to the Basin for their school sports. Handicap races were popular, so the starting area was marked off in grids of one yard. An official, resplendent in white trousers and blazer, positions the small boys on their marks. The groundsman's shed and the play area identify the site in the south-west corner of the ground.

Stewie Dempster (below) was born in Wellington in 1903 and grew up living in Kent Terrace, so the Basin Reserve was where he played, summer and winter.

The short, stocky Dempster had hardly reached his mid-teens when he was hinting at prodigious cricket talent. He joined the Institute club when it did not have a senior side, a situation Dempster soon helped rectify. In one season of lower grade cricket, he scored nine centuries and a 99 in 10 innings. He entered senior cricket as a 17-year-old and enjoyed the same sort of success. Eventually in club cricket he scored 7,813 runs at 75.8, with 30 centuries, five of them doubles. He is the outstanding batsman in Wellington club cricket history.

In his 10 tests, Dempster scored 723 runs at 65.72. Of batsmen who have played 15 test innings, Dempster's average is second, behind that of a chap named Bradman, and ahead of Sid Barnes, Graeme Pollock, George Headley and Herbert Sutcliffe.

He made two tours of England, leading the averages both times. In 1927, he scored 1,430 runs at 44.7. In 1931, he scored 1,778 runs at 59.3 and was named one of *Wisden*'s five players of the year. Dempster then accepted an offer by furniture magnate Sir Julien Cahn and based himself in England, qualifying for and captaining Leicestershire in the county championship.

DON NEELY COLLECTION

DON NEELY COLLECTION

In six straight seasons he averaged 40 or more, three times over 50.

New Zealanders got another glimpse of Dempster in 1939, when he combined a tour with Sir Julien's team with his honeymoon. He played the one international of the tour, at the Basin, and made 44. After the war, he had a couple more seasons of Plunket Shield cricket. Though into his 40s, he scored well. In 1946–47, he made centuries against Canterbury and Auckland and was selected for New Zealand 14 years after his last test. An eye injury forced his withdrawal.

Dempster's return to the capital helped rejuvenate cricket in the area. He gave coaching clinics and lec-

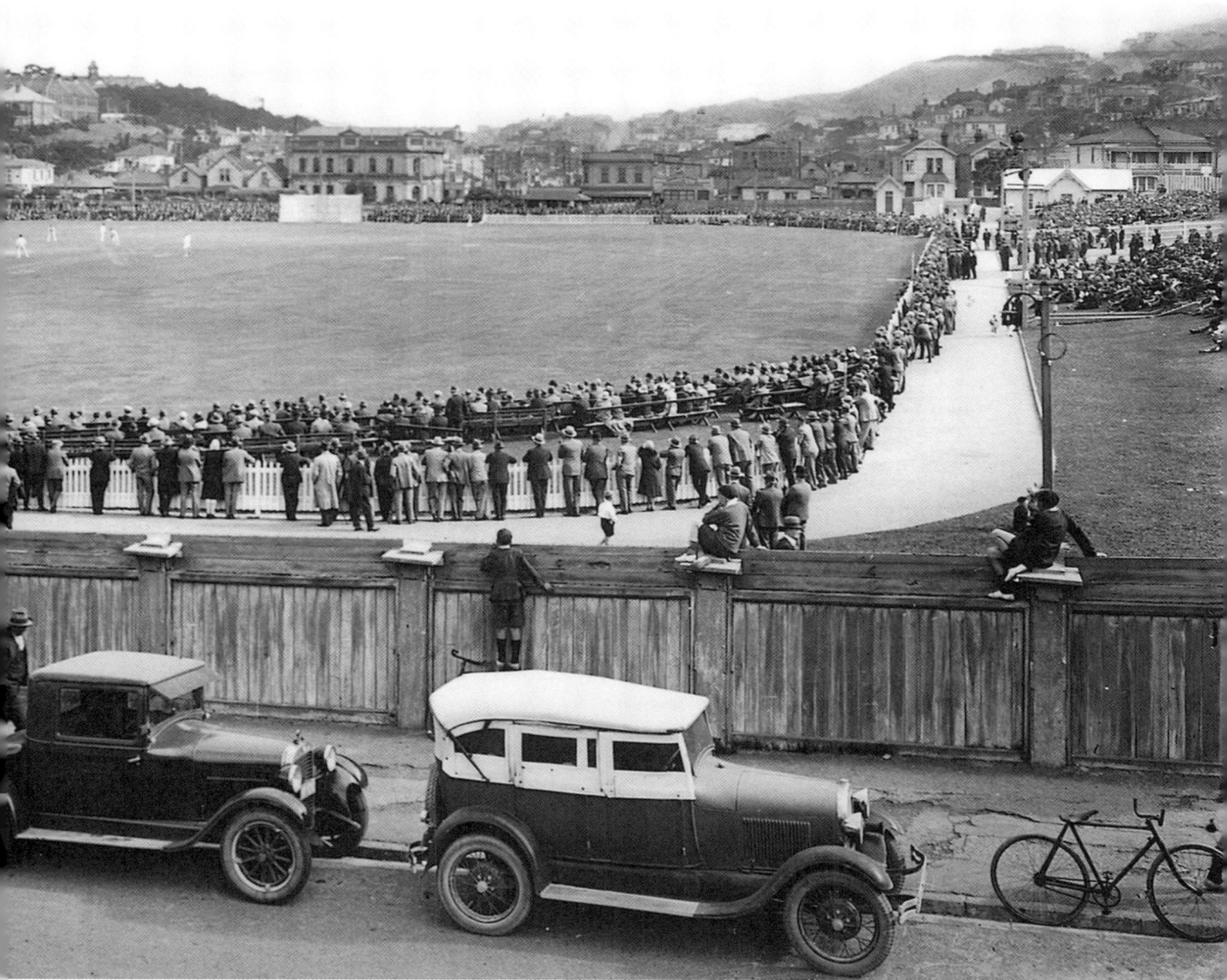

tures and did a regular cricket session on radio. He moved to Auckland shortly after and lived there for nearly 20 years.

When Dempster eventually shifted back to the capital, he was asked by Wellington Cricket Association chairman Rob Vance to become involved in coaching again and so returned to the Basin 60 years after he had played there as a child. This time he helped a group of promising youngsters with some sage advice. Bruce Edgar, Robert Vance and Evan Gray were three who had much for which to thank the elderly gentleman with the kindly manner. Between them, they played 326 games for Wellington.

▲ New Zealand v. England, 24 January 1930. This was an historic occasion in the story of the Basin Reserve, for it was the first cricket test played at the ground. The Basin thus became the world's nineteenth test venue. By 2002, 81 grounds had hosted tests. The 1930 match, which was drawn, was enriched by a 276-run first-wicket stand by New Zealand openers Stewie Dempster and Jack Mills, who scored the first test centuries for New Zealand, with Dempster reaching the mark first.

The motorcars of the day look resplendent parked along Buckle Street. Only a very optimistic bicycle owner would leave his bike leaning against the footpath these days and expect it to be there at the end of the day's play.

Herb McGirr (right) was one of the most popular characters from the first golden age of Wellington cricket. Wellington won the Plunket Shield five times in nine years from 1924, and did so with a core of outstanding players. Besides McGirr, there were Stan Brice and Sid Hiddleston (in the early years), Stewie Dempster, Ken James, Tom Lowry, Ted Badcock and Jack Lamason, all New Zealand representatives.

McGirr was a vigorous, hard-hitting batsman and a right-arm medium-pace bowler. He was a gritty, determined cricketer who thrived on a battle. But he was also a person who seemed to attract colourful stories.

In 1924, when Wellington played New South Wales, champion Australian leg-spinner Arthur Mailey offered him a cigar for every six he hit. After debating with Mailey the quality of the cigars on offer, McGirr hit four balls out of the Basin Reserve on his way to a thrilling 92. One of them went through a window of the Caledonian Hotel. The proprietress told the fieldsman retrieving the ball that he couldn't have it. She would deal only with McGirr. The game continued with another ball. When McGirr went to the hotel afterwards, the proprietress flung her arms around him and said the hit through her window was the best advertisement the hotel had ever had.

McGirr scored 3,992 runs in first-class cricket at 28.71 an innings and took 239 wickets at 27.49. He

had just one test, against England in 1930 (though he toured England under Tom Lowry in 1927). In it he scored 51 in his one innings and had bowling figures of 1–115. He would have loved the fact that his test batting average put him in the elite 50-plus category and would have smiled, too, at a bowling average that placed him among the real part-timers.

After leaving Wellington in 1932, McGirr was Nelson College coach and groundsman for many years.

This wrestling match from the early 1930s has drawn a good-sized crowd. The photo, buried deep in the Alexander Turnbull Library archives, contains minimal accompanying information but is a reminder about the remarkable variety of sports the Basin Reserve has hosted down the years.

▲ The Basin Reserve during the winter of 1931, with two soccer pitches. Note the jumping pit in the foreground.

▼ The groundsman rolls a pitch in preparation for another round of club matches in 1932. The worn patches where clubs used practice wickets can be seen at each end. A six-lane running track has been marked at the northern end. The large bare space above the Basin, formerly occupied by the Mount Cook Barracks, has been cleared. The Dominion Museum would be built there in 1936. The Carillon is on the right.

▶ The Basin Reserve and its surrounds, pictured from the newly erected Carillon, which was opened on Anzac Day 1932. Note the Mount Victoria Tunnel, completed the previous year. Wellington East Girls' College has not yet been completed. The Wellington College cricket pavilion was built in 1924.

To mark his appreciation of the success of the New Zealand team's 1927 tour of England, businessman Eric Riddiford donated £250 to build a scoreboard and scorers' box on the eastern side of the ground.

DON NEELY COLLECTION

◀ Assisted by two of his pupils, Alf Jenkins, whose Jenkins Gym was a landmark in Wellington for decades, demonstrates strength and balance during a gymnastics exhibition at the Basin Reserve in the early 1930s.

▼ A sight to gladden any cricket administrator's heart. Patrons queue outside the northern end of the ground, all eagerly anticipating action in the 1933 international between Wellington and England. Rain confined the match to just one day, during which England made 223–8 declared and Wellington replied with 141–2. England's star batsman Walter Hammond made 58, and team-mate Eddie Paynter 52, while for Wellington Stewie Dempster scored 47. People dressed more formally in those times, but the weather must have been brisk that morning – most of those in the queue are wearing coats, and women have fox furs.

A crowd of 25,000 flocked to the Basin Reserve on Sunday, 25 February 1934, to celebrate the diamond jubilee of Archbishop Redwood, who is pictured above arriving at the ground with due pomp and ceremony. At right he is pictured saying Mass at the Basin Reserve from an altar-like baldachinum (a canopy over a throne) built in front of the grandstand.

The archbishop was born in England in 1839 and his family moved to New Zealand in 1842. He entered the priesthood in 1865, and in 1874 became the youngest bishop in the world. By the time of his diamond jubilee, he was, at 95, the world's oldest archbishop.

The scenes of celebration from 25 to 28 February were remarkable. They included a procession by 10,000 Catholics that was more than a mile in length as it moved from the Basilica of the Sacred Heart in Hill Street to the Basin. Over the next two days, the Archbishop visited the Otaki Catholic Maori Mission and St Patrick's College, Silverstream.

Archbishop Redwood estimated that from 1865 to 1934 he had celebrated more than 24,000 Masses.

WELLINGTON SOCCER ASSOCIATION

Errol Holmes's 1935–36 MCC team played four 'tests' on their tour of New Zealand. The fourth, in Christchurch, was ruined by rain and abandoned early.

To fill in time, the MCC cricketers met Wellington in a soccer match at the Basin Reserve. It was a cold day, but a crowd of nearly 3,000 attended. Wellington won 5–2, but the visitors were not outclassed by the locals. They had in Yorkshireman Wilf Barber and Nottinghamshire's Joe Hardstaff two men who could have made a living from soccer if they had not preferred cricket.

An intriguing member of the MCC side was the Honourable Charles Lyttelton, who was to succeed to the title of Lord Cobham and serve as New Zealand's Governor-General from 1957 to 1962. The second 'test', at the Basin, was noteworthy because one of New Zealand's opening bowlers was Wellingtonian Denis Blundell, who was to serve as Governor-General from 1972 to 1977. What a coincidence having two future Governors-General oppose each other in a cricket international only a few metres from Government House!

The MCC team provided Wellington cricket fans with a highlight. Wellington beat the visitors by 14 runs – a better result than New Zealand could manage in the four-match series that season. The home-town hero was Blundell, who took 5–50 to help bowl out the MCC for 130 in their second innings.

ALEXANDER TURNBULL LIBRARY

Shortly after his famous 1936 Olympic gold medal run at Berlin, Jack Lovelock toured New Zealand, giving running exhibitions and making speeches. Here he jogs a lap of the Basin Reserve with some local runners. Lovelock drew crowds of several thousand at most stops on his tour. People were content just to see him wearing his New Zealand uniform and running lightly.

New Zealand's match against Sir Julien Cahn's team, played at the Basin Reserve 10–13 March 1939, was notable for a number of reasons. It was the last time two fine players, Sonny Moloney (left) and Bill Carson, represented New Zealand. Both were to die while serving overseas during the second World War. This was the only match in which great left-hander Martin Donnelly represented his country at home and the only occasion that pace bowler Tom Pritchard played for New Zealand.

The touring side was captained by Nottinghamshire captain George Hearne and included England batsman Joe Hardstaff, Australian left-arm spinner Jack Walsh and New Zealand expatriate Stewie Dempster. After the first two days were rained out, New Zealand, captained by Moloney, made 170–5 declared and Cahn's team were 163–7 in reply at stumps.

Richie Romanos (left) was born in Belfast Street, across the road from the Basin Reserve, in 1928, and lived there throughout his childhood. He was one of many children who used the Basin as their playground in those days. 'Our video shop,' was how another well-known Wellingtonian, Spiro Zavos, described it.

Romanos attended St Joseph's School and St Patrick's College, and played soccer and cricket at the Basin, and competed there in the McEvedy Shield athletics. He later played Plunket Shield cricket for Wellington briefly, his first match, in 1951, being at the Basin.

But in reality young Richie was fortunate to survive childhood after some of the antics he got up to at the Basin. One particular scheme that could have resulted in his death was pigeon-hunting. 'We had a neighbour who would pay me half a crown for a bag of pigeons. That was good money for a youngster in the 1930s, and I was game,' he recalls. 'So I'd climb up onto the roof of the old grandstand and clamber along, grabbing the pigeons that were perched there. I would stuff eight or nine under my jersey, then climb back down.

'Sometimes I would crawl under the roof and walk along the wire netting to catch them. This was a bit more dicey because the wire netting was rusty and sometimes my foot would slip through. It wasn't hard actually catching the pigeons. They just stood there. It was getting to them that was tricky.

'When I think back, it was terribly dangerous. I was only about 10 and I'd climb up at night, or in the rain, and would be wearing ordinary shoes. One day the groundsman, Budge Brewer, a very nice man, saw me. He couldn't believe his eyes and told my mother. He said to her that if I fell, he'd be using the wheelbarrow to pick up all the pieces. My mother was horrified and I was told in no uncertain terms that my pigeon-hunting days were over!'

Some fine athletics was seen at the Basin Reserve during the war. Within the space of six weeks in early 1940, there were four major meetings held on the Basin – a Canterbury v. Wellington meeting on 28 January (won by Canterbury 16 events to 9), the Grand Centennial Sports Gathering on 10 February, a professional Centennial Championship meeting on 16–17 February and the Centennial national championships on 8–9 March.

The first meeting included leading athletes of the day like Colin Dickie, Doug Herman and Bill Pullar, and drew a good crowd. The professional meeting was a combination of athletics, cycling and woodchopping and it was felt that the novelty of the woodchopping events was the reason for the 3,000-plus crowd. The woodchoppers competed for cash, and Dinny Hoey was a tremendous attraction, with Merv Jensen and Whata Green also shining. The cash cyclists turned on a display of high-quality riding, with the Sutherland brothers, of Christchurch, particularly impressive. Unusually for a mixed sports meeting, the athletics events attracted least interest – few good athletes in 1940 were prepared to surrender their amateur status even with the prospect of picking up useful cash prizes.

It was the Grand Centennial athletics meeting and the national championships that captured the public imagination, especially as they featured two memorable mile races. The first, and most famous, took place during the Grand Centennial meeting. This was an exciting time for miling in New Zealand, and athletics officials briefly entertained the thought of having a New Zealand team attempt to break the world four by one-mile relay record.

For this race at the Basin, the country's leading milers were brought together: Dickie, the Wellington one-mile champion; Ces Matthews, the 1938 Empire Games three- and six-mile gold-medal winner; Pat Boot, the Empire Games half-mile gold medallist; Spencer Wade, a former national mile champion; and Pullar, who had not only twice won the New Zealand mile title, but was also a four-time national cross-country champion.

Dinny Hoey in action at the Basin Reserve.

SPENCER WADE COLLECTION

Colin Dickie leads Ces Matthews, Pat Boot, Spencer Wade and Bill Pullar in the 'Mile of the Century'.

Unfortunately, the race was held in heavy rain, which affected the time, though not the quality of the racing. Boot won in 4 minutes 15.8 seconds, just two seconds outside Randolph Rose's national record. Wade was second in 4 minutes 17 seconds. 'I made my bid going down the final back straight and led with about 150 yards to go,' recalls Wade, 'but Boot, who was New Zealand's pre-war Snell, cut me down in the final straight.'

Dickie, who died in 2001 aged 81, remained involved in athletics long after his running days were over. For several decades, he was the starter at most major athletics meets in Wellington, including many at the Basin, and was the chief starter at the 1974 Christchurch Commonwealth Games.

The 'Mile of the Century', as it was labelled, made a tremendous impression on the 4,900 Wellingtonians present. Peter Sellers was a young man at the time, but says he wouldn't have missed the race for anything.

'There was talk about it for days,' says Sellers. 'Colin Dickie made the pace up to the bell lap. Boot challenged and went past. Then Matthews chased Boot, who eventually pulled away. The time was pretty good considering they were running in torrential rain and it was on grass. It started raining at 2.15 p.m. that day and just got harder and harder. By the time the mile began, at five past three, it was coming down in sheets

and we couldn't even see the runners when they were on the far side of the track.'

As with most sports meets at the Basin in this era, the programme comprised a mixture of cycling and athletics events. While the mile was the feature, there was a full programme of cycle races, an inter-sports club relay race (featuring teams from Waterside Workers Cricket team, Huia Hockey Club, Watersiders' Association Football Club, the Government Printing Office Sports Club and the Petone, Athletic, Varsity and Wellington Football Clubs), and a marching display by the New Zealand Royal Air Force Band.

A month later, the athletes and cyclists were back again for the national championships. It was much the same cast and again the mile was the feature event. This time Pullar won from Len Dickison, of Otago, and Wade.

Other competitors that year included Empire Games javelin gold medallist Stan Lay, Ernie Todd of future rugby fame (he won the discus), future Wellington rugby coach Clarrie Gibbons (who ran in the marathon) and in the cycling events, Alvin Pennington, who would become the long-time organiser of the Auckland to Wellington cycle race.

The game of softball originated in the United States in 1887, and 50 years later arrived in New Zealand when expatriate American staff introduced it to workers at the Ford Motor factory in Lower Hutt. From there it spread to nearby Wellington, where men like Alf Jenkins, the country's best-known wrestling referee, and Benny Wilson enthused over the new recreation.

As early as 1939, the first national interprovincial tournament, with the Beatty Cup at stake, was held, with Canterbury winning the title.

Over Easter 1940, the Basin Reserve hosted six provinces – Auckland, Mana-watu, Wanganui, Wellington, Canterbury and Otago. Three matches were played at 10 a.m. The semi-finals began at 11.30 a.m., with one winning side getting a bye to the final, which was played at 3.15 p.m. Auckland beat Wellington 20–0 in the final.

The photo above shows Canterbury at bat on their way to a win over Wanganui.

Since 1940, the Beatty Cup has become one of the major sports events of the New Zealand summer. The tournament stretches over nearly a week now and has been played all around the country. Softball has developed enormously in New Zealand, helped by the Black Sox, as they are now called, several times winning the world crown.

Wellington and Hutt Valley have generally been the softball strongholds, but Southland, Canterbury, Hawke's Bay, Waikato and Auckland have all produced champion teams.

Theodore Wright Leslie was one of the big names of Wellington sport. Dorrie Leslie, as the world knew him, was born in 1870 and was a good athlete. In 1892, in a race at Feilding, he was timed at 6 minutes 23 seconds for the one-mile walk, equalling the world record.

But Leslie was to earn his place in sports history not as an athlete, but as a trainer and a race starter. He trained champions in many sports, ranging from the All Blacks, to wrestler Georges Hackenschmidt, to champion boxers, to swimmers and athletes.

One of his best-known pupils was swimmer Bernard Freyberg, who went on to win acclaim in many fields, and to be New Zealand's Governor-General from 1946 to 1952. Speaking at the Wellington Town Hall during the early years of the Second World War, Sir Bernard noticed Leslie in the front row and said, 'I see my old trainer down there. He was a hard taskmaster, but he made a man of me.'

In 1904, Dorrie Leslie spent a week training the New Zealand rugby team at a camp in Days Bay. He must have done some good, for they beat Great Britain 9–3 at Athletic Park. Leslie often spoke admiringly about the champions in that team – Dave Gallaher, George Nicholson, Billy Wallace, Duncan McGregor, Charlie Seeling, Billy Stead and Fred Roberts.

Leslie continued coaching the All Blacks, as they became known. There was another camp at Days Bay before New Zealand drew 3–3 with the Anglo-Welsh in June 1908, and he was still the All Black trainer before they took on the Springboks in the decisive third match of the 1921 series. He recalled Alf West of Taranaki arriving at that camp with his belongings tied in a handkerchief. That match, played in torrential rain, was drawn 0–0. His last association with the All Blacks was in 1923, when he prepared them to meet a strong New South Wales team.

As a famous trainer, and as the custodian of the Wellington Town Hall from 1904 to 1935, Leslie was well known, but it was his skill as a race starter that really kept him in the public eye. He started races at virtually all major meets in New Zealand for 45 years and was the starter at the 1932 Los Angeles Olympics. Leslie was extremely popular with children, who used to crowd around him as he started races at the Basin Reserve and Athletic Park. He would always give

ALEXANDER TURNBULL LIBRARY

one of them the used shell after he had started a race.

He had an unusual style. He was the first starter to hold the gun well above his head, instead of behind his back, when giving the starting instructions. He figured that if there was any problem with the timekeepers hearing the shot, they would see the puff of smoke when he fired. At first, some people felt Leslie was showboating, but in time all starters came to adopt his method.

Leslie continued to be involved in all major athletics meets at the Basin through the Second World War and after until his death in 1950.

Waterside, of Wellington, became the first team to complete a hat-trick of Chatham Cup victories when they beat Mosgiel, of Dunedin, 6–2 in the 1940 final at the Basin Reserve. Their previous two victories were 4–0 against Mosgiel in 1938, and 4–2 against Western, of Christchurch, in 1939.

Eight of the Waterside team played in all three finals – goalkeeper Sid Ward, fullback Bob Bolton, centre half Fred Hazel and the entire forward five of Colin McCarthy, Tom Walker, Sonny Ward, Alf Longbottom and Toby Janes. Ward scored in all three matches.

The 1940 final was played on a firm ground in sunny conditions before 8,000 spectators. Mosgiel scored in the second minute, but after that it was a decidedly one-sided contest with the experienced Waterside team dominating.

In the photo above, Alf Longbottom, in the distinctive Waterside black-and-white stripes, follows up a shot that Mosgiel goalkeeper A. Hall appears to have covered. Watching developments is Mosgiel's centre half H. Mills, while referee J. Graham is excellently positioned to judge if the goal is scored.

SIX

The Basin's Heyday
1941–1960

THE BASIN RESERVE was in its heyday in the 1940s and 1950s as a centrally located multi-purpose venue able to cater for night sport, a rarity at the time. A staggering number of sports were played there in these two decades.

Cricket continued its dominance at the Basin. Apart from the Plunket Shield and other domestic matches, teams from Australia, England, Fiji, South Africa and the West Indies all played at the Basin. Cricket followers thus got the chance to watch a mouth-watering array of household names, such as Ray Lindwall, Bill O'Reilly, Keith Miller, Len Hutton, Denis Compton, Alan Davidson, Clyde Walcott, Everton Weekes, Gary Sobers, Frank Worrell, Peter May, Neil Harvey, Richie Benaud, Jim Laker and Fred Trueman.

Tom Pritchard, an outstanding pace bowler from Taranaki, then Manawatu, played just one game for New Zealand, against Sir Julien Cahn's team at the Basin in 1939. He later forged a successful professional career in England.

However, another Pritchard performance at the Basin gained more headlines. In a North v. Central Army match in the 1942–43 season, he captured 10–39 and, remarkably, bowled nine batsmen and had the tenth, Auckland batsman Alf Postles, lbw. For that feat, he was given a set of pipes.

A keen follower of sport in Wellington for many years has been Dan Kelly. On Pritchard's great day, he was a pupil at St Patrick's College. Sitting in class, he could see the first part of Pritchard's run-up and then his view would be obliterated by a building. He recalls watching eagerly and seeing the run-up begin, then a pause, then the roar signalling another wicket.

As early as the 1920s, some YMCAs held sports carnivals between business houses and other groups, and these included marching displays. However, marching began formally in New Zealand during the Second World War. The disciplines of war, plus the dearth of summer team sports for girls, led to its organisation as a recreation and then, in August, 1945, to the formation of the New Zealand Marching and Recreation Association. The sport quickly took hold and the first New Zealand championship was held in Timaru in 1946.

Englishmen Len Hutton (left) and Denis Compton stride out to resume battle during the 1951 test at the Basin. Hutton, the world's best batsman at the time, made 28, and Compton, who had had a poor tour of Australia, returned to form with a delightful 79. The test was drawn. Between them, Hutton and Compton scored 240 first-class centuries, 36 of them in tests.

Wellington became a stronghold for marching, and the Basin was the marching centre of Wellington, hosting several national championships, various international events and other marching exhibitions. By the mid-1950s, there were 360 teams competing throughout New Zealand. Marching remains the only major sport invented by New Zealanders.

The national athletics champs were held at the Basin in 1945 and 1951. There were many other big athletics occasions at the Basin. A host of international stars competed, some complaining about the wind and/or the uneven surface, but most showing the stamp of class.

Caribbean sprinters Lloyd laBeach and Herb McKenley, and New Zealand's own champions such as Yvette Williams, Doug Harris, Dutch Holland, Val Young, Marise Chamberlain, Murray Halberg and Les Mills all competed at the Basin. The weather wasn't always kind. LaBeach and McKenley arrived amid tremendous expectation in 1949, for in those days anyone either American or connected with America was a glamour figure. But the two sprinters struck an ugly Wellington day, dark and grim. Even though it was an afternoon meeting, it was hard to distinguish between them when newspapers published photos of their race the following day.

Rugby league was played at the Basin occasionally. Wellington took on visiting teams from Britain, France and Australia and there was a smattering of internationals, too, including an historic win by the Kiwis over Australia in 1953.

Soccer continued to use the Basin extensively and after the Chatham Cup resumed following the Second World War, every final was played there through this

In December 1951, Wellingtonians got a sneak preview of the explosive sprinting of Australian Marjorie Jackson, who was to win the Olympic 100 metres / 200 metres double at the Helsinki Olympics the following year. 'The Lithgow Flash', as she was dubbed, was in a class of her own at the Basin, turning her 100 yards and 220 yards races into exhibitions. Of all the fine Australian sprinters who ran at the Basin, none, not even Betty Cuthbert or Judy Pollock, impressed more than Jackson.

During the Second World War, many schools and public places had air-raid shelters built. The Basin Reserve was no exception, and members of the public, plus school-boys from St Pat's and Wellington College, assisted in the digging of the shelters, in the north-west corner of the ground, where the R. A. Vance Stand is to be found now.

period. All New Zealand's leading players appeared at the Basin, including Dennis Charlton, Ken Fleet, Bert Hiddlestone, Don Kendrick, Dave McKissock, the goal-scoring wizard Jock Newall, Charlie Steele, Jim Stephenson, Phil Traynor and Ian Upchurch.

One occasion of note occurred on Saturday, 4 August 1945, when famous English singer Gracie Fields kicked off in the Chatham Cup Wellington semi-final between Marist and Seatoun. It was a bitterly cold, windy day and the rain belted down. In fact, it was so cold that the other soccer game scheduled for the Basin that afternoon was abandoned after some players were taken from the field suffering from hypothermia. Despite the atrocious weather, a sizeable crowd turned out to see the English star. Proceeds from the day went to the Gracie Fields Charitable Trust for sick and wounded servicemen in New Zealand. Fields appeared wearing black jersey, white shorts and football boots under her oilskin coat. She made a short speech and then, though she could hardly move in the thick mud, kicked off into the wind before returning to the pavilion. Marist won the game 5–0 but, three weeks later, lost the Chatham Cup final 4–3 to Western of Canterbury.

Nor was the big soccer at the Basin limited to the Chatham Cup. There were club and provincial matches and some internationals, too. In 1947, New Zealand (this was 34 years before anyone had conceived of the name the All Whites) played their first post-war match, beating Wellington 5–2 at the Basin. Two years later, New Zealand received two 4–0 hammerings at the Basin from a strong Australian side. During the 1950s, New Zealand turned out at the Basin to play Victoria, Wellington, Hong Kong and Australia. That 1958 match against Australia was a beauty. It attracted a big crowd and although New Zealand lost 3–2, they showed signs of the form that would bring them a draw and a win in the other two matches of the series. Big Ken Hough, a former Australian (and a New Zealand test cricketer) was in goal for New Zealand.

Sports such as cycling and boxing made occasional appearances. Cycling was often linked with athletics in combined sports meetings and, as well, the national grasstrack championships were held twice at the Basin in this period.

Boxing's big day came in 1954 when the hugely popular welterweight Barry Brown cheered the hearts of locals by winning his Empire title fight against South African Gerald Dreyer.

▶ 8 May 1945, the war in Europe is finally over and VE Day celebrations are held at the Basin Reserve.

Hockey continued to use the Basin for many of its biggest matches. Wellington played internationals against Australia in 1948, losing 3–1, and in 1952, when the game was drawn 0–0. A brilliant Indian Wanderers team toured New Zealand in 1955, easily beating Wellington in muddy conditions at the Basin. Also, in 1948, an Australian women's team beat Wellington 5–1.

Softball was played at the Basin under lights for several years in the 1950s, when night games helped to enhance and publicise what was then a fledgling sport.

There were novelty sports events, too. The Harlem Globetrotters turned up at the Basin in 1957, the same year as Sam Snyder brought his famed Water Follies to the ground. It is hard to conceive of today, but a basketball court was laid for the Globetrotters and full swimming and diving pools were set up for the Water Follies.

A solemn crowd of soldiers, sailors, Wrens, airmen and citizens of Wellington gathers in front of the Basin Reserve grandstand to mark VE Day. In the distance, younger people climb the slide for a better view. The Boys' Institute, which many people attended for coaching in all sports, is further to the south along Tasman Street.

All sorts of band exhibitions have been held at the Basin, plus several national band championships. In 1945, 500 bandsmen delighted a crowd of 10,000, despite rain that set in. A big attraction was the Wellington Ladies' Highland Pipe Band, making their public debut. Other bands involved were the Caledonian Highland Pipe Band; the Police Highland Pipe Band; the Pipes and Drums, the 1st Battalion, the Wellington Regiment; the Scots College Pipe Band; the Hutt Valley Highland Pipe Band; the Hutt Valley High School Band; the Trentham Camp Band; the Boys' Institute Silver Band; the Hutt Civic Band; the Hutt Municipal Band; the Tramways Band. Trumpeters from Wellington Technical College opened proceedings with a ceremonial fanfare.

Another occasion at the Basin that had a tremendous impact was the massive celebration there on VE Day 1945.

Various exhibitions, ranging from balloonists to helicopter landings took place and each invariably drew several thousands of spectators. On weekends, bands would often use the Basin to practise their routines, and these provided nearby citizens with an afternoon of free entertainment.

The area surrounding the Basin changed. An earth-

In 1942, Robert Vance helped Wellington College to their win over Silverstream at the annual McEvedy Shield meeting by taking first place in the shot put and the discus (above). Vance later captained Wellington in first-class cricket and became chairman of Wellington and New Zealand Cricket. In 1981, the new stand was named in his honour. Note the signs of the trenches dug into the bank on the right and the army huts in front of the grandstand.

quake during the Second World War damaged the Caledonian Hotel, causing the top storey to be removed. This didn't worry the owners too much – they made bigger profits from selling alcohol than letting rooms. To the north-west, St Joseph's School and the Home of Compassion next door to St Patrick's College moved. Patterson Street was extended and now ran west from the tunnel to the Basin, meaning motorists no longer had to make a curious detour to Ellice Street when emerging from the tunnel.

There were still periodic calls for the Basin Reserve to be demolished to make way for improved roading, just as others demanded that the Basin's facilities be upgraded. The Director of Parks and Reserves, E. Hunt, was quoted in 1948 as saying: 'The Basin Reserve pavilion is in an extremely neglected state, having apparently had very little – if any – maintenance since it was erected.' The 1954 royal visit provided the biggest impetus of the period, leading to the installation not only of floodlighting, but also of a paved walkway in front of the old grandstand, and increased seating capacity on the western side. Though the Basin gradually aged and its facilities became tired and rundown, it was still the major sports ground in the capital. In the days before Wellington had its Westpac Stadium, the Newtown Park all-weather athletics track, Rugby League Park or the Queens Wharf Events Centre, the Basin was *the* sports venue. Wellingtonians had cause to venture there several times a year and the ground, so near to the central city, was dear to the hearts of the locals.

A champion announces his arrival. It's December 1943, Auckland v. Wellington. Auckland made 438–7 declared, an innings dominated by a spectacular 146 by 20-year-old left-hander Bert Sutcliffe, who was soon to confirm his class with brilliant innings all around New Zealand and overseas. It was an interesting match. Wellington, following on nearly 300 behind, fought back after being 62–6 in their second innings. Wicketkeeper Frank Mooney played his best innings, making 180 and added 127 for the ninth wicket with Ray Buchan and 113 for the 10th wicket with Diddy Knapp. Auckland eventually won by eight wickets.

The Wellington fieldsmen are, from left: Ernie Bezzant, Frank Mooney, Bill Dustin, Ray Buchan, George Dickinson, Diddy Knapp, Eric Tindill, Bob Menzies, Merv Pengelly (umpire), Gilbert Stringer, Ray Allen and Ces Muir. The Auckland batsmen are Len Kent and Brian Sorenson.

Note the dodgems and other carnival entertainment set up on the eastern side of the Basin Reserve. It might have been the middle of the war, but a carnival atmosphere existed at the ground. Left-arm spinner Ray Allen might not have appreciated it on that day – Sutcliffe made a habit of hitting him into the dodgems!

Winston McCarthy (right) was the prince of radio rugby commentators. He broadcast the Kiwi Army team's matches in Britain, France and New Zealand in 1945–46 and covered All Black tours of South Africa (in 1949) and Britain and France (in 1953–54), besides the big matches at home until after the 1956 series against the Springboks.

No-one could make a rugby commentary come to life like 'Wee Mac', as he was known. He made the rugby incredibly exciting for the fans at home. Who could forget his 'Listen . . . it's a goal!'

But McCarthy was more than a rugby broadcaster. During the Second World War, he was the ground announcer/broadcaster for nearly all the major athletics meetings held at the Basin Reserve. McCarthy watched a young Doug Harris clean up every event from the sprints to the 800 metres at a Combined Services meet at the Basin on 17 April 1943 and told listeners that New Zealand had unearthed a future Olympic champion. Harris might have fulfilled McCarthy's prophesy but for an untimely Achilles' tendon injury during the 1948 London Olympics.

McCarthy broadcast other sports at the Basin, including rugby league and hockey, and would broadcast cricket from a converted van that had previously been used by air-traffic controllers and was parked beside the sightscreen at the northern end of the ground. It was a strange-looking van, with a Perspex dome protruding from the top.

The idea was that McCarthy would be able to look out through the dome, thereby being able to broadcast in relative silence. But he used to swelter on hot days and would open the Perspex top. This made life more comfortable for him, but it meant cricket spectators even quite a distance away could hear his commentaries.

While McCarthy made the cricket exciting, he wasn't always entirely accurate. Sometimes a group of young children would linger beside the van and scoff at him loudly when he described a flowing cover drive as the ball scudded towards fine leg.

Eventually, when he knew he was about to go on air, he would call over the youngsters and implore them to let him commentate in peace. After a while he even took to bribing them with bags of sweets so that they would not favour the listening thousands with their views on his commentaries.

Neville Colvin's view of the strange-looking commentators' van, as published in the *Sports Post*.

The first cricket test between Australia and New Zealand began on 29 March 1946 and didn't actually achieve test status until two years later – the match was billed merely as an 'international'. The brilliant visitors overwhelmed New Zealand, winning inside two days, and Australia did not play New Zealand in another official test for 28 years.

New Zealand, caught on a difficult Basin wicket, were bowled out for 42 and 54 and lost by an innings and 103 runs. The New Zealand batsmen were unable to cope with the accuracy of Ernie Toshack and Bill O'Reilly in particular, and only Merv Wallace, with 10 and 14, managed double figures in each innings.

The match provided New Zealand with its first taste of test cricket for nearly nine years and drew big crowds on both days. One who was there was nine-year-old Don Neely, who two decades later would captain Wellington to victory in the Plunket Shield. 'I remember slipping out the northern end of the ground on the first morning to buy some fish and chips across the road,' Neely recalls. 'The shop was busy and I found myself struggling to be served before a seemingly never-ending stream of adults. When I emerged, I saw that we had been dismissed for 42. At the time I thought the New Zealand team would be very pleased. After all, only a few days earlier my Miramar School team had been dismissed for 33 and we had been warmly congratulated by our coach!'

New Zealand's dismal showing provoked a poem by Temple Sutherland, of Nelson ▶

TEN FOR FORTY-TWO
(A Lament)

TEN little wickets, guarded by our best Eleven,
    Anderson let Lindwall through – and 1 was down for 7.
NINE little wickets standing on the Basin Green,
    The Skipper fell to Toshack, 2 down, the runs 15.
EIGHT little wickets, but we're sorry to relate,
    Toshack collected Wallace; 37 on the slate.
SEVEN little wickets when Scott of Auckland came,
    But O'Reilly sent him homeward, the score, alas, the same.
SIX little wickets, and with Rowe, O'Reilly proved
    He could keep the batsmen moving – so the score remained unmoved.
FIVE little wickets, but O'Reilly never faltered,
    Butterfield pokes his leg before, the score remains unaltered.
FOUR little wickets and O'Reilly to McRae, Hassett
    takes it single-handed, the score just stays that way.
THREE little wickets, New Zealand's 'thin red line'
    Burke – leg before – bowled Toshack, 8 down for 39.
TWO little wickets wishing hard that they were more,
    Toshack skittles Tindill – and 40 is the score.
ONE little wicket on which our hopes depend,
    Tallon says 'good-bye' to Cowie, and at 42 – the end.
NO little wickets, but still a record score.
    We have never made so little in so big a game before.

Keith Miller displays great agility to catch Walter Hadlee at leg slip, watched by Sid Barnes, Ian Johnson and wicketkeeper Don Tallon. Note the list of the fielding side on the scoreboard. A bulb would light up when the player fielded the ball.

▲ An important athletics meeting held often at the Basin was the annual McEvedy Shield contest between all the major boys' colleges in the greater Wellington area and beyond. In the 1940s, Hutt Technical College, Hutt Valley High School, Rongotai College, Scots College, St Patrick's College, St Patrick's Silverstream, Technical College, Wairarapa College, Wellesley College and Wellington College all competed. McEvedy Shield day was invariably a big one for local sport.

The combined pipe bands of Wellington and Scots Colleges lead the parade of competing athletes before the start of the 1947 McEvedy Shield.

A large number of future sports stars took part in this inter-school athletics competition. In the mid-1940s, Hutt Valley High School fielded two future superstars, cricketer John Reid and All Black Ron Jarden, in their team. Strangely, Reid ran in the sprints and Jarden in the 440 and 880 yards.

▶ Until the 1951–52 season, there were only four first-class teams contesting the Plunket Shield. Players from Taranaki across to Hawke's Bay, and south to Nelson and Marlborough could play first-class cricket only for Wellington.

Each season during the 1920s, '30s and '40s, a trial match was played over two days at the Basin Reserve between Town and Country. Neville Colvin's *Sports Post* cover of 7 December 1946 captures the tone of the game.

DON NEELY COLLECTION

During the 1947–48 season, the Fijian cricket team toured New Zealand, playing 17 matches, including five three-day games that four decades later were designated first-class. The big-hitting tourists, dressed in their traditional cricket garb of salu skirts and with bare feet, proved extremely popular with spectators, none more so than Bula, whose spectacular and unorthodox hitting brought him 1,011 runs during the tour at an average of 37.44.

When Fiji met Wellington from 27 February to 1 March, it was Bula, with a powerful 88, who spearheaded Fiji's chase of 247 in the fourth innings. In a thrilling finish, Fiji got there with one wicket to spare. The Wellington team was a strong one, including test players Eric Tindill, Trevor Barber, Eric Dempster and Frank Mooney and also the big-hitting Kilbirnie player Stewie Wilson, always a crowd favourite.

IHC ARCHIVES

For many years, the Parents' Association of the Intellectually Handicapped Children searched for a site to establish an occupational centre. On 26 April 1950, the Leader of the Opposition, Peter Fraser, headed a deputation to the Minister of Education, suggesting that a temporary centre be established in the Basin Reserve pavilion. The Minister agreed.

A month later, the parents brought their children to the pavilion, but through lack of communication it had not been prepared. The centre eventually catered for 24 children, who on fine days were able to enjoy the play area beside the pavilion. The temporary measure lasted until the IHC opened a new occupational centre in Coromandel Street in 1952.

The OSH people today might raise an eyebrow, but the play area provided children with decades of fun.

The most remarkable result in the history of the Chatham Cup occurred in 1949 when Petone, of Wellington, beat Northern, of Otago, 1–0 in the final at the Basin Reserve. It looks a typical soccer scoreline, but there was a wonderful story behind it.

There was never a collection of cup winners like the Petone Settlers. Earlier in the year, Andy Leslie, Peter McVean and Jim Campbell, all veterans of the 1928–30 cup-winning sides, had headed to the immigrants hostel at Fort Dorset, Wellington, to recruit potential Petone players. The Wellington association deemed that the new team would play in the second A championship, effectively the capital's third division.

Leslie, assisted by Campbell, coached the side, and McVean was manager. Petone began their cup campaign against a strong Marist team and won 7–1. Railways and Institute followed as victims. Then Petone met the previous year's finalists, Waterside, in the Wellington final. It took two games and two 1–1 draws before a lone corner took the Settlers to Ohakea and a 2–0 provincial final success.

On Petone battled. Next they travelled to Auckland, where Eden hosted them at Blandford Park. After 90 minutes of normal time and 40 minutes' extra time (no golden goals and penalty shootouts in those days), bad light stopped play with the score 2–2. Petone won the replay in Wellington 2–0.

Against the odds, they were in the Chatham Cup final. More than 12,000 turned up at the Basin on a chilly August day for the final. After a sluggish start, Petone dominated the second spell. When that excellent goalkeeper Jim Stephenson blocked Dave McKissock's shot, Wally Hewitt tucked the rebound away for the winner. Petone keeper Ben Savage then played his part by saving a penalty.

An overflow crowd, well wrapped up to combat the cold, eagerly waits for the 1949 Chatham Cup final to begin.

'The family that prays together stays together' was the creed of American priest Father Patrick Payton, who drew overflow crowds throughout his tour of New Zealand in March–April, 1954. Some 25,000 people turned up at the Basin Reserve on Sunday, 4 April, to hear Father Payton say the Rosary. Hundreds of Wellington schoolchildren formed the shape of a rosary around the ground.

RESERVED
BLOCK E

In the 1950s, when things American fascinated New Zealanders, the visit of the US carrier *Tarawa* in May, 1954 excited colossal interest. Thousands of Wellingtonians took the opportunity to inspect the massive ship, and the American sailors made quite an impact during their time in the capital. They gave a musical concert at the Town Hall and took part in an exhibition softball match.

Another activity that interested Wellingtonians was the helicopter display at the Basin. It was advertised that a helicopter from the *Tarawa* would hover over the ground and demonstrate how to winch up a person. There was a hitch when the person nominated to be winched was late arriving, so local radio identity Haydn Sherley was pressed into action.

'I didn't have time to think about it,' says Sherley. 'They sent down the rope from the helicopter, I was hitched up and they began hauling me up. After a few seconds I got a bit cocky and stopped holding on, but there was a jolt and I grabbed the rope for dear life. I suppose they lifted me 50 or 60 feet.'

DAVID TOSSMAN

One of the most eagerly awaited sports contests at the Basin Reserve during the 1950s was the rugby league match on 8 August 1953 between Wellington and an American All Stars team. In the programme for the Wellington v. Auckland league clash at the Basin the previous year, it was written: 'Considerable interest is being aroused by the proposed visit of the American side next season . . . The rugby league code has in the past couple of years taken firm root in the United States with California as its headquarters . . . early indications suggest that the United States is liable to be a serious contender for world supremacy.'

These comments were wildly exaggerated, though an American team, assembled by Mike Dimitro, did duly visit in 1953.

The American All Stars were strengthened by the addition of outstanding Kiwis Des Barchard, Travers Hardwick, Roy Roff and Frank Mulcare. The tourists played eight games in New Zealand, winning three.

Their match at the Basin drew a good crowd of 5,000. Radio journalist Peter Sellers recalls: 'The spectators loved the Americans' gear. They looked like Flash Gordon. The big attraction was simply that they were Americans. Anything American back then had appeal – whether it was their ships visiting our harbours or their sports teams arriving. Wellington were captained by Morrie Church and won 18–17. It was a lot of fun. There were guys running around with long pants, shoulder pads and helmets. Each American footballer looked like the Michelin tyre man!'

PETER KERRIDGE COLLECTION

Mike Dimitro (left) and his American All Stars.

The Basin Reserve was a happy hunting ground for rugby league in the decade after the war. The most significant result was the 12–11 win over Australia in 1953 when Bob Neilson scored near fulltime and ever-dependable place-kicker Des White converted to wrap up the test match and the series. On a badly cut-up ground, New Zealand, who had won the first test 25–5, trailed 2–8 at the interval. But the Kiwi forwards lasted better and gradually pulled their team back into the match. In five decades since, New Zealand have not won another series against the Kangaroos. This was the last league test played at the Basin.

The other notable test victory at the Basin was the 26–21 win over Australia in 1949, when West Coast forward Charlie McBride crashed over for the vital try. It was a golden era for New Zealand league, with stars like White, Tommy Baxter, Ron McKay, Morrie Robertson, Bill Sorensen, Jimmy Haig, Cyril Eastlake, Frank Mulcare, Bill McLennan and McBride all household names.

New Zealand captain Jim Haig manages to clear the ball. Other Kiwis in this photograph from the 1953 test at the Basin are Jimmy Edwards, Alister Atkinson and Bob Neilson.

The installation of floodlights at the Basin Reserve opened the way for a considerable amount of night sport. A midweek Hutt Valley v. Wellington soccer series was played under lights and marching, athletics, boxing and basketball were tried at night at the Basin. Possibly the most successful venture was night softball, which took place for several seasons from 1954. Softball players and officials relished the opportunity to showcase their sport by staging club matches during summer evenings.

Future Wellington representative Garry Ward recalls his first game of senior softball under lights: 'I was at centre field and couldn't see any ball hit above the level of the floodlights. It was a matter of watching where the ball went, positioning yourself where you hoped it might come down and reacting quickly when it came back into view. Modern softballers would think the conditions were a joke – there was no way you could see a speed pitcher like Bill Massey. The softball diamond faced away from the grandstand. It was lined up from the clock, so a hit to left field headed towards Kent Terrace. The games used to draw several hundred people at least. Admission was five shillings or so, to cover the cost of the floodlights.'

Change Of Plans For Basin Reserve's New Seating

In 1950, the Wellington City Council was criticised for the way it administered the Basin Reserve. The council got it from both ends – some said being devoted to sport wasted such an ideally located amenity. Others claimed the council was remiss in not building better grandstands and other amenities.

A few years later, the Basin was in the news again when Harold Austad, chairman of the New Zealand Olympic and Athletic Associations, returned from England determined that the Basin should be upgraded into a world-class track and field facility. Having attended an athletics meeting at London's White City, Austad called for a cinder track to be laid and for the ground to be enclosed to cut down the wind.

While Austad's bright hopes were eventually dimmed, there was progress at the Basin in the 1950s. In 1953, plans were unveiled for the ground to be floodlit to allow night sport. An *Evening Post* report of 8 October 1953 detailed how there would be 48 lights, at a cost of £7,000. The lights, installed on four 60-foot steel latticed towers, would be the equivalent of 720 normal streetlights and would give Wellington the best floodlit ground in New Zealand. It was hoped that soccer, using a white ball, would be played there.

In August 1953, plans were finalised to extend the concrete seating in front of the grandstand, increasing the capacity to about 2,000. Work was given urgency because of the planned royal tour of New Zealand in January 1954 by the newly crowned Queen Elizabeth II. As a newspaper report noted: 'The seats will be for the aged or sick who would otherwise have little chance of seeing the Queen.' By October, things were humming and workmen prepared for the pouring of the concrete (left). The floodlights and concrete seating were ready by December 1953.

The Basin remained the focus of well-laid intentions. In 1956, the city council had plans to build a stand at the Kent Terrace end of the ground at a cost of £120,000, but the project did not proceed.

Through 1953–54, welterweight boxer Barry Brown was a huge drawcard, pulling sellout crowds everywhere. Promoters, seeking to increase spectator capacity, scheduled his Empire title fight against South African Gerald Dreyer for the Basin Reserve under lights, on 15 January 1954.

There had been boxing before at the Basin. A local trainer had used a room under the main stand as a temporary gym during the early 1940s and at Easter 1943, the Basin hosted a programme of Army bouts, matching leading amateurs like Bos Murphy and Jack McCann against American Marines, the pick of whom was Abbott Carlisle. A curious aspect of this fight afternoon was that the amateur boxers did not wear singlets.

The Brown v. Dreyer fight was a much bigger occasion. It cost the Wellington Boxing Association £8,000 to stage the fight. Dreyer was on a guarantee of £2,000, plus return air fares for himself and trainer Teddy Bentham. The association gambled by charging £2 15 shillings as its ringside ticket price, a huge sum, and the cheapest seats cost 10 shillings. This proved too expensive for many fight fans, and the crowd, expected to be 15,000, was just 5,000 on the night.

Sir Robert Jones, just a teenager but already passionate about boxing, and Barry Brown in particular, recalls that Dreyer held particular appeal because he was a 1948 Olympic gold medallist, had fought in America and had a world ranking.

Brown was an unusual boxer. He would shadow box in his mind, so for three minutes he would stand in one place, arms held high, twitching this way and that. His hobby was knitting. His supporters were a diverse group that included politicians like Keith Holyoake, clergy and many women (who paid halfprice to attend boxing in those days).

The ring was set up in front of where the R. A. Vance stand is now. Peter Sellers recalls that the lights in the grandstand were turned on and that a tarpaulin suspended above the ring also had lights attached.

Bentham was a big name in boxing and nearly 20

NEW ZEALAND FREELANCE, ALEXANDER TURNBULL LIBRARY

Barry Brown (left) evades Gerald Dryer's left hook.

years later was to be chief second for Jerry Quarry when he fought Muhammad Ali in Atlanta in Ali's comeback fight. Queen Elizabeth and the Duke of Edinburgh were in Wellington at the time of the Brown v. Dreyer bout. There was talk that the Duke, a boxing fan, would attend, but he did not.

Brown dominated the fight, knocking down Dreyer twice before referee Phil Stone stopped the bout midway through the seventh round. There was euphoria from the crowd, who, almost on cue, sent their green plastic seat cushions – purchased at the venue before the fight – sailing into the ring in celebration after Brown's victory. The cushions were purchased for one shilling and therefore were known as 'Bob Comforts'.

▶ New Zealand cricket administrators today wouldn't mind crowds like this for three-day matches. On the Saturday of the Wellington v. MCC match in 1955, the largest crowd ever to watch a cricket match at the Basin Reserve – 18,139 – gathered to see Wellington take on the team that had successfully defended the Ashes in Australia. Tom Graveney made a century for the tourists and left-arm spinner Johnny Wardle bowled well, but the local team performed above expectations, particularly bowlers Bob Blair, Eric Dempster and John Reid. The MCC won by 187 runs.

DON NEELY COLLECTION

NEW ZEALAND FREELANCE, ALEXANDER TURNBULL LIBRARY

The New Zealand grasstrack cycling championships are no longer held, but for decades were an important part of the national calendar. The Basin Reserve occasionally hosted the event. In this picture, taken during the 1957 nationals, Warren Johnston, of Waikato, powers into the straight in the one-mile event. Johnston, one of New Zealand's finest cyclists, swept the 880 yards, mile and three-mile titles during the meeting.

Everybody who follows basketball knows about the Harlem Globe-trotters. These brilliant American professional basketballers/entertainers were formed in 1927 and have made more than a dozen exhibition tours of New Zealand. Wellington venues they have played at include what used to be Central Park (now the Renouf Tennis Centre) and the Winter Show Building.

On 16 and 17 January 1957, in the heart of the cricket season, the Harlem Globetrotters played two matches at the Basin Reserve against their perennial rivals, the Hawaiian Surfriders. The ever-popular Americans left a host of memories.

Robin Fordham, then just a schoolboy, remembers: 'The Globe-trotters romped home as everyone expected and wished. There was a lot of humour in the game. Once, by clever handwork, the real ball was replaced by an identical one made of bread, and at the vital moment, the Globetrotters began to tear the ball to bits and eat it. It was a thoroughly enjoyable fun event.'

Peter Sellers recalls the impression the all-black team made: 'There was no television in New Zealand back then, and we weren't used to seeing a team of huge black men. They were a very big attraction. The Harlem Globetrotters all had great flair, but one player, James Harrison, stood out – he was extremely agile and fast, and very funny.

'They always started their show with their signature tune, "Sweet Georgia Brown". It was all very professional. They brought their own compere, whose commentary was funny and informative, and when they finished they signed autographs. It was a family show with a real gala atmosphere.'

Another spectator was Garry Ward. 'The emphasis was really on entertainment,' says Ward. 'There was a carnival or mini-circus before the basketball match, and it included a high-wire walker. The American announcer talked about the danger the tightrope walker was facing because of the "ferocious winds", when we all thought it was a very mild zephyr.

'The court was set down directly in front of the grandstand. It was a portable wooden court and was placed over the grass. The players didn't really like it because they said they couldn't get much bounce owing to the grass underneath. They brought their own lights. I remember it as a very exciting night.

'There was a lot of interaction between the players and crowd, with things like staged player protests at referee decisions. They would pretend to throw water over the crowd, but confetti would come out of the bucket . . . that sort of thing. But besides all the antics, the Globetrotters played some wonderful basketball. They were really super athletes.'

JOSEPH ROMANOS COLLECTION

DON NEELY COLLECTION

Through the 1950s and early 1960s, Wellington fast bowler Bob Blair ruled supreme at the Basin Reserve. Blair was superbly fit and could bowl for long periods. On the Basin wicket, with a strong breeze at his back, he was at his lethal best. He could make the ball lift sharply off a length and worried all but the greatest batsman. Many a batsman spent an uneasy night knowing he would have to face Blair on the Basin the next day.

Blair averaged five wickets in an innings once every two games, a remarkable strike rate. His total of 329 wickets for Wellington established a provincial record that has been bettered only by Ewen Chatfield and Evan Gray, who played considerably more matches. Blair's most remarkable season was 1956–57, when he captured 49 wickets in five matches at an average of 12.24. Twice within three matches at the Basin that season he captured nine wickets in an innings.

Few events at the Basin Reserve required the planning of the two Water Follies shows in March 1957. Sam Snyder's troupe had toured the world since 1946, giving water ballet and diving exhibitions. The 1957 divers included Barbara McAulay, the 1954 Empire Games gold medallist, and tower diver Stanley Mitchell. The shows also featured the Gorgeous Aquabelles, a 16-woman precision swimming team, Eddie Rose, 'the world's greatest water comedian', balancing acts, dancing, singing and Chet Clark, 'the virtuoso of the harmonica'.

Equipment had to be imported into New Zealand under special licence. The diving pool was 50 feet long, 35 feet wide and 8 feet deep. The second pool, used by the water ballet and exhibition swimmers, was 75 feet long, 35 feet wide and 5 feet deep. It required 50,000 gallons of water to fill the pools.

Peter Sellers, one of 10,000 people who attended the shows, says it was top-class entertainment: 'They placed the pool and stage in front of the grandstand, on the walkway between the picket fence and the seating. It had rained for the five days before the Water Follies arrived, but both shows were held in the evening in good weather. The sound system was extremely good for those days and Eddie Rose was particularly popular. I thought the synchronised swimmers were terrific. This was years before there was any thought of it going into the Olympics.'

The photo below of the portable pools used at the Basin is taken from the programme.

PETER SELLERS COLLECTION

In March 1957, New Zealand took on a strong Australian cricket team. In the second 'test', at the Basin Reserve, New Zealand had the better of the match. Bert Sutcliffe graced the game with an elegant century.

There was much interest in the comparison between Sutcliffe and Australian Neil Harvey, two of the world's great left-handed batsmen. Sutcliffe won this private battle easily, for the Australian made just two and three.

The Australians resorted to leg theory to try to quell Sutcliffe. Here he misses a hook off Ron Gaunt's bowling and the ball flies down the leg side to wicketkeeper Barry Jarman. Peter Burge and Richie Benaud field at leg slip. The other batsman is Don Taylor and the umpire is Jack Cowie, one of New Zealand's finest pace bowlers.

A canvas sightscreen is tied to the boundary fence at the southern end. To the left, the commentary box housed a technician, a scorer and two commentators.

Wellington clubs enjoyed much success in the Chatham Cup through the 1940s and 1950s. Marist, after a heart-breaking 4–3 loss to Western, of Canterbury, in 1945, won in 1946. Then Waterside, Petone and Stop Out claimed titles. In 1957 and 1958, it was Seatoun's turn. They swamped Christchurch City 7–1 in 1958, a record margin in which centre forward John Donovan scored six goals. In a team stacked with talented players such as Gordon McClelland, Ron Kearns, Neil Kerr, Keith Gibson, Bill Logan and goalie Bert Hiddlestone, it was incredible that Donovan would so dominate.

Seatoun's 3–1 win over Technical, of Christchurch, the year before (pictured at right) was harder-earned. The young Seatoun team owned much to Bill Logan, who scored twice.

From left: Ted Charlton (Technical), Vic Smith (Technical), Keith Gibson (Seatoun), Bert Hiddlestone (Seatoun), Brian Fletcher (Seatoun), Andy McAnulty (Technical) and Ernie Fields (Technical).

AFTER P.H. STANDIDGE'S PERFORMANCE, AND JOHN REID'S HURRICANE HITTING, AGAINST WANGANUI LAST WEEK, IT WOULDN'T BE SURPRISING —

SPORTS POST

CRICKET
HUTT VALLEY
v.
W'GTON
AT THE
BASIN
RESERVE
29 NOV 6.00.

"YES, WE DO GO PAST THE BASIN RESERVE."

BRYAN WADDLE COLLECTION

Paul Standidge was a pugnacious left-handed opening batsman who believed most bowlers should be hit to – and over – the boundary. On 27 November 1958, he found himself in a situation that was tailor-made for his big hitting. His Karori club side were chasing 145 runs in 72 minutes against Wellington College Old Boys on the Basin Reserve No. 2 wicket, on the eastern side of the ground.

Early in his innings, Standidge smashed a ball over the scorers' box into Dufferin Street. Fieldsmen jumped the fence but couldn't find the ball. Some small boys bore witness to the fact that the ball had hit a passing tramcar. And so it had.

It transpired that the ball had smashed through the glass of the route indicator and lodged in the box and wasn't found until the tram arrived at the Island Bay terminal.

Some Wellington cricketers believed this might qualify as the longest distance a cricket ball had ever been hit.

Marching girls from 27 teams form a 'W' (for Wellington) on the floodlit field. The formation was the culmination of an evening of marching and band performances at a

1959 Festival Tattoo, watched by a crowd of 6,000. In the background, canvas covers protect the wicket to be used the next day in the England v. Wellington cricket match.

EVENING POST

For more than a quarter of a century the annual James Smith's Christmas Parade began outside the Basin Reserve and wound its way along Cambridge Terrace and through Courtenay Place to James Smith's. The parade drew thousands of spectators along the route. The Santa float, always a highpoint of the spectacle, departs from the Basin Reserve on a rocket in the 1959 parade.

New Zealand waited years to unearth a genuinely fast bowler. While New Zealand batsmen had to cope with the likes of Lindwall and Miller, Tyson, Trueman and Statham and Adcock after the Second World War, New Zealand could not find anyone of true express pace until 1960. That's when 19-year-old Gary Bartlett was introduced for three internationals against a strong Australian combination. What an impact he made! In his first effort for New Zealand, at the Basin Reserve on 19–23 February 1960, Bartlett took 5–51, including the wickets of Australian captain Ian Craig, Bobby Simpson and Grahame Thomas. He bowled with terrifying pace throughout the series, claiming 12 wickets. He made Craig's life a misery, dismissing him five times.

Bartlett never quite kicked on. He suffered injuries, and opposing batsmen, perhaps seeking to gain a psychological edge, suggested that he threw. However, nothing can diminish the memory of the sight of the young Bartlett steaming in to bowl at the Australians at the Basin. After his first delivery, John Reid and the rest of the slip fieldsmen took three paces backwards.

Dick Brittenden, New Zealand's pre-eminent cricket writer, recalled that series with a smile. He spoke of a world-class player like Simpson being all at sea, playing and missing.

It's hard to believe, looking at this 1960 aerial photo of the Basin Reserve in winter
(note the two soccer fields), taken from above Courtenay Place, that just over a
century earlier, there had been plans for the Basin to be a harbour and for Kent
and Cambridge Terraces, in the centre foreground, to be a canal along which
barges would be drawn by horses towards the Basin.

SEVEN

Television Takes Control
1961–1981

THE BASIN RESERVE grew tired during the 1960s and 1970s. Facilities such as players' changing rooms, public toilets and the grandstand, which were hardly acceptable decades earlier, were now simply not up to international standard. As always, there was much debate about what should be done with the Basin. Much of the uncertainty was caused by roading requirements, with the Wellington City Council seeming to alter its thinking on this issue regularly.

At a council meeting on 19 April 1961, it was discussed, without any dissenting voice, that the Basin be sold. The councillors were informed that it would solve traffic problems and that an elaborate sports ground would be built, some day, at Kilbirnie.

An *Evening Post* editorial the following evening attacked 'selling the city's birthright', accusing the council of taking leave of its senses. 'Citizens will be aghast at its incredible decision provisionally to abandon the Basin Reserve as a sports ground and thus rob Wellington for all time of one of its greatest assets,' said the editorial. It called on 'all sportsmen, beautifying societies and all who cherish a love for nature, who believe that no city can be complete unless it has within a minimum of open spaces for rest and recreation' to write in condemnation of the proposal.

The controversy died but was rekindled two years later when the American engineering company of De Leuw, Cather and Company was commissioned by the city council to prepare a comprehensive transportation plan for Wellington.

When it was released in August 1963, the plan called for the closure of the Basin. The Foothill Motorway Plan, as it was called, proposed an additional tunnel through Mount Victoria to cope with the four-lane construction from Ghuznee Street to the tunnel, with an interchange at the south end of Cambridge Terrace,

circling over the area where the R. A. Vance stand is today, as well as requiring the demolition of the old grandstand.

A direct north–south road was proposed to extend between Cambridge Terrace and Adelaide Road. For several years newspapers were inundated with letters debating the plan.

The 1963 Foothill Motorway Plan that would have spelt the end of the Basin Reserve.

DON NEELY COLLECTION

The appointment of Ian Galloway as director of parks and reserves brought a council rethink and a decision on the motorway was deferred until 1980. Galloway spent $14,000 on a new fence, and new rooms were created inside the grandstand, which was also repainted. The press box by the eastern scoreboard was enlarged and the scoreboard repaired. Work was carried out on the field, where the undulating surface made fielding a nightmare.

But this was no more than a holding operation and finally, late in 1978, work began on the Basin, which underwent its most significant changes in appearance since the 1855 earthquake. It was reshaped, fitted with an impressive new scoreboard at the southern end and a spectacular new stand in the north-west corner, named after leading cricket administrator Rob Vance. The Basin was transformed from a drab looking sports ground into one of the most modern, eye-catching cricket arenas in the world, one that uniquely combined the modern and the quaint.

Soccer enjoyed some great times. The Chatham Cup final continued to be played at the Basin, often in chilly, raw weather. Every final has its own story, but Hamilton Technical's 4–1 win over Northern of Otago in 1962 is rated one of the best finals ever. Equally well remembered, but for a different reason, is the 1971 wind-dominated final, when Western Suburbs beat Wellington City 3–2.

In addition, soccer's national league was launched in 1970 and Wellington teams played some entertaining matches on the Basin. The Wellington teams in the league varied through the years, but in the 1970s they included Hungaria, Stop Out, Wellington City, Wellington Diamond United (who won the title in 1976) and Waterside.

After the first cricket test was played at the Basin Reserve in 1930 – and ended in a draw – the ground hosted only another five tests over the next three decades, and all five were lost by New Zealand. But their improvement at international level was illustrated at the Basin in the two decades after that: New Zealand played nine tests and lost only twice, winning three and drawing four.

The most convincing of these victories occurred on 17 February 1976, when they beat India by an innings and 33 runs. It was New Zealand's ninth test win and their first by an innings.

The game was notable for the bowling of Richard Hadlee, who announced his arrival as a world-class cricketer by taking 7–23 in the second innings – still the best bowling figures by a New Zealander in a test at home.

In the photograph above, Hadlee leaves the field to the applause of his team-mates, a sound he was to hear often over the next 15 years. From left: Mark Burgess, Bhagwat Chandrasekhar (the last Indian batsman), John Parker, Andy Roberts, Richard Hadlee, Dayle Hadlee, Bevan Congdon, Richard Collinge, Ken Wadsworth, Glenn Turner and John Morrison.

ALEXANDER TURNBULL LIBRARY

Among the overseas soccer teams to play at the Basin, the most popular was the 1961 England side. Three hours before kick-off, more than 2,000 people were inside the ground. The grandstand had been sold out several weeks before, as had a special tubular stand between the grandstand and the open seating. Every available vantage point was taken, including the roof of the groundsman's shed.

New Zealand played a smattering of internationals at the Basin, the most famous being the clash with England in 1961. Other visiting teams included Luton, New Caledonia, Wolverhampton Wanderers and China.

An England B team that toured in 1978 was a big attraction, outplaying New Zealand 3–1 at the Basin. Bobby Robson, later to be England boss, managed the tourists, who won the three tests that season. New Zealand acquitted themselves best at the Basin, holding England scoreless through the first half. The game marked the international debut of Bobby Almond, who was named Man of the Match and paid $50 for his efforts. Brian Turner scored New Zealand's only goal of the series, chipping England goalie Joe Corrigan.

Most of the leading players of the period – including Ken Armstrong, Brian Turner, Earle Thomas, Steve Sumner and John Houghton – represented New Zealand at the Basin.

Marching, with the brilliant Lochiel team supreme, was a regular attraction in this period. There were New Zealand and North Island championships at the Basin and, in 1977, the first Inter-Dominion championships, won, not surprisingly, by Lochiel.

The last hockey test played at the Basin was on 1 July 1961, when an Indian Wanderers men's team beat New Zealand 3–1. Wellington continued to play matches against touring sides, and in 1967 an Australia men's team beat Wellington 3–1 in front of a surprisingly big crowd.

The ground's days as a major athletics venue drew to a close in the mid-1960s. But in 1961, cashing in on the 1960 Olympic gold medal successes of Peter Snell and Murray Halberg, New Zealand athletics officials organised an international tour, sponsored by Agfa. The series wound up on a windy night in Wellington, where Halberg beat American Dyrol Burleson over a mile in the feature race, while Snell repeated his 1960 Olympic triumph by beating Roger Moens over the half-mile. Other leading New Zealand athletes who competed included Barry Magee, Gary Philpott and Bill Baillie.

The weather was again far from balmy the following year when the international tour again stopped off in Wellington, though that did not deter 8,000 spectators from attending. The big draw was Snell, who in the previous fortnight had run world records for the one mile, 880 yards and 800 metres. There was some excellent

127

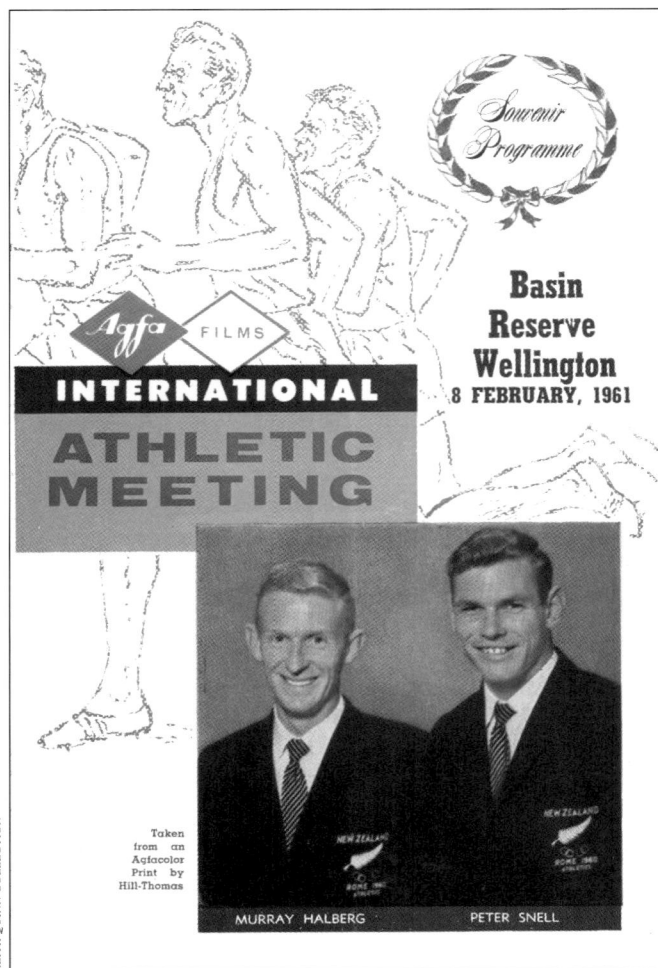

Souvenir Programme

Basin Reserve Wellington
8 FEBRUARY, 1961

Agfa FILMS

INTERNATIONAL ATHLETIC MEETING

Taken from an Agfacolor Print by Hill-Thomas

MURRAY HALBERG   PETER SNELL

racing, despite a strong wind. Halberg held off the rising John Davies and Dave Karl in the mile, Englishman Bruce Tulloh won the two miles from Magee, and Snell outsprinted Americans John Bork and Ernie Cunliffe in the half-mile.

Rob Mitchell, a cricket administrator for 25 years, remembers the night well. He was a member of the Hutt Valley YMCA gymnastics team who were exhibiting their prowess on the horizontal bars in the middle of the ground. During one of the major races, one of the bars came out of the ground while Mitchell was on it and he was tossed on to the grass.

There was one more major international meeting, in 1966, when overseas stars included Ralph Doubell, George Kerr, Irina and Tamara Press, and Judy Pollock. After that, the Basin hosted the occasional McEvedy Shield meeting but little else in the way of track and field events.

There was the odd big rugby league match in the 1960s, such as when Wellington took on British sides, or, in 1963, South Africa, but the New Zealand Rugby League preferred to allocate tests to Auckland or Christchurch. Rugby League Park came into being in 1970, and that virtually spelt the end of the Basin as a league venue, though in 1975 New Zealand and Wales met under lights at the Basin in a World Cup match.

Cricket, as always, was the major sports attraction at the Basin. A win over Dennis Silk's MCC side in 1961

One Wellingtonian who made a welcome reappearance at the Basin in the 1970s was Denis Blundell, who played 19 games for Wellington from 1930 to 1938. He returned to the Basin on 23 December 1972 and met the Auckland and Wellington teams in the opening Plunket Shield match of the season. By then he was His Excellency the Governor-General of New Zealand, Sir Denis Blundell, GCMG, GCVO, KBE. Sir Denis thoroughly enjoyed mixing with old friends. From left: Breeze Airey, Sir Denis, Rob Vance and, obscured, Jumbo Symes.

EVENING POST

During the 1974 football season, a hot-air balloon was launched from the Basin.

might not seem so special now, but was a significant milestone for New Zealand cricket. Barry Sinclair, diminutive and precise, scored buckets of runs in club cricket and made a memorable 148 against a strong Australia B side in 1967. Twelve of the Australians were or became test cricketers.

Ironically, considering the Wellington v. Australia B game ended in a high-scoring draw, the New Zealand Cricket Council took away the unofficial test from the Basin that season and played it at Pukekura Park, New Plymouth, where New Zealand won a famous victory. The Basin lost its host rights because of the unsatisfactory wickets at the ground over the previous two seasons

– created mainly by successive layers of top-dressing converting a flat playing surface into a rolling paddock. The day after the game against Australia, the city council parks and reserves department arrived at the Basin and bulldozed the ground flat.

In 1969, the Basin was the setting for a hard-fought six-wicket test win over the West Indies. The Chappell brothers, Ian and Greg, both scored a century in each innings of the test in 1974, a unique feat. Four years later, Richard Hadlee captured 10–100 and Richard Collinge 6–77 (including the prized scalp of Geoff Boycott twice) to bowl New Zealand to an historic victory over England.

SO EARLY IN THE SEASON, NOT EVERYONE CAN BE EXPECTED TO BE FIT —

BUT THERE IS   ONE MAN   WHO REALISES —

THAT THE MORE   OTHERS ARE   NOT FIT, —

THE MORE   HE'LL BE RUNNING.

PEEP PEEP PEEP

ORDER OF ST JOHN, WELLINGTON

For three decades *Evening Post* cartoonist Nevile Lodge entertained Wellingtonians with his whimsical views on sport, sportsmen and things Wellington. In many of his drawings were to be found members of the Order of St John helping players overcome all manner of injuries. These good Samaritans spent hours huddled on the sidelines, and were affectionately known as the 'Zambucks'. The senior man was dressed in a black uniform with a black cap, his female assistant in a grey uniform and hat. Invariably they had a young cadet in black with short trousers.

From the 1940s into the 1970s, the senior Zambuck at the Basin Reserve was Corporal Frederick Mintey. No matter how adverse the weather, he would be there. The Basin was his ground and the chocolate-maker from Adams Bruce Ltd was in charge.

The most celebrated soccer match at the Basin Reserve in this period occurred in 1961 when New Zealand were pummelled 8–0 by an England side studded with big names. New Zealand trailed only 2–0 at halftime, but the superior fitness of the visitors helped them score four goals in the final 15 minutes. The English were a mix of amateurs and professionals, led by one of the all-time greats, Tom Finney, and including a young fullback named Bobby Moore, who five years later would captain his country to World Cup glory. New Zealand were captained by Jim Warrender, and Ken Armstrong was player/coach.

The Englishmen, who had earlier beaten Canterbury 11–1, travelled from Wellington to Auckland and won the second test 6–1.

Below, Englishman John Farlow, who scored two goals, contests a ball with Ken Armstrong.

EVENING POST

► In 1963, South Africa's rugby league team made their only tour of New Zealand and proved surprisingly popular. They met Wellington at the Basin Reserve on Thursday, 1 August 1963, and won 21–12. The day was drab, with a strong, cold southerly. A few days later, South Africa handled the mud better at Auckland's Carlaw Park to upset New Zealand 4–3.

At right, Wellington winger Robin Strong dives over the shoulder of South African winger Johnny Gaydon. Following up from left are Jim Andrews and John Rasmussen.

▼ Groundsman Doug Kelly (left) and former test umpire Merv Pengelly roll the wicket for the game between New Zealand and Australia A in March 1970. The macabre sight of a dead seagull hanging from a pole by the pitch was a common one at the time – it used to keep live seagulls off the area. Not only did Kelly have to prepare a test wicket, he also had to ready the ground for two days of intercollegiate athletics just before the international.

131

A cricket world record was created at the Basin on 15 January 1963 when John Reid hit 15 sixes in his innings of 296 against Northern Districts. Reid, pictured below during his innings, began the second day 0 not out and in 144 minutes before lunch, scored 174. Twice he hit the ball over a 10-metre high fence into the front field of St Patrick's College, a carry of at least 100 metres. His innings had an unusual effect on the spectators, who, after the sixth six, realised they were witnessing something special. Each six after that was greeted by laughter verging on hysteria. There was a carnival atmosphere at the Basin that day. Reid's 296 was scored in 220 minutes. The next highest Wellington score was 24, made by Paul Barton.

Reid was the special hero of the Basin for nearly two decades. He was a towering figure in New Zealand cricket from 1948 to 1965 and chose the Basin for many of his greatest feats, including:

- His 283 against Otago in 1952, including 41 fours.
- A devastating bowling spell of 7–38 against Canterbury in 1959. Canterbury needed just 116 to win, but Reid single-handedly deprived them of victory.
- A punishing 191 not out to guide Wellington to victory against the clock over Northern Districts in 1959.
- Leading New Zealand to victory over Dennis Silk's MCC team in 1961. Reid paved the way for the one win in the series, at the Basin, with a virtuoso all-round performance.

Reid played 44 of his 246 first-class matches at the Basin. In addition, he played memorable innings in minor rep games and in club cricket at the ground. Besides his powerful strokemaking, Reid was also a class bowler, brilliant fieldsman, handy wicketkeeper and, from the early 1950s, generally the captain of any team for which he played.

His association with the Basin continued when he had a second stint as a national selector in the 1970s. He was as proud as anyone that historic day in 1978 when New Zealand finally managed to beat England for the first time in a test. When he was finished playing and selecting, Reid became one of the International Cricket Council's first match referees.

During the 1950s Reid was employed by the Wellington Cricket Association as its coach, and in 1963 built a commercial squash complex in Kelburn.

Of all the many fine Wellington players, few have had the magnetism of Reid, and it was fitting when the J. R. Reid Gate at the southern end of the ground was named in his honour.

On 16 December 1968, plans were unveiled for an exciting new stand at the Basin, to be built on the corner of Rugby and Sussex Streets in the south-west corner. The stand was to accommodate 500 members of the public and 400 members of the Wellington Cricket Association. For a subscription of $20, members would have use of seating, a Long Room modelled on Lord's, with full bar facilities and a dining room, and a members' lawn in front of the stand.

Two indoor nets were to be built underneath the stand. New premises for the media were to be built in one of the five high towers that were a striking feature of the design, submitted by architects Calder, Fowler and Styles. The estimated cost was $371,500. It was intended to extend the pavilion down the western side of the ground.

The existing stand was perceived to have outgrown its effectiveness and the council was concerned with the increasing maintenance costs. A large car park was to be built in the vacant area when the old stand was demolished. The proposal did not get further than the drawing board.

DON NEELY COLLECTION

On 11 March 1969, New Zealand achieved their first cricket test victory at the Basin Reserve after a fiercely contested match with the touring West Indies team, led by Gary Sobers. It was the eleventh test played at the ground since 1930. Previously, seven had been lost and three drawn.

Dick Motz, the Canterbury pace bowler, captured six wickets on the first day to give New Zealand the advantage. During this spell, he established a test mark for New Zealand by taking his tally to 86 test wickets, bettering John Reid's 85.

Above, Motz is pictured receiving the congratulations of his team-mates. From left: Bryan Yuile (glasses), Motz, wicketkeeper Barry Milburn, Ross Morgan, Graham Dowling, Bevan Congdon, Vic Pollard and Glenn Turner.

EVENING POST

For the first time in almost 85 years, alcohol was allowed to be sold at the Basin Reserve when the West Indies and New Zealand met in 1969. The proviso was that patrons did not take the paper cups or cold cans outside the area fenced off with hessian.

Spectators quickly dubbed it the 'beer bank garden'. On a sunny first day, 4,800 cans were sold. On the second day, a beer tanker was brought in to meet the demand. At police insistence, by 12.15 p.m. the licensees were forced to shut down after selling a further 1,200 cans. The licensing committee's first condition had been broken – patrons had been taking the beer outside the enclosure.

The photo above shows the ground enclosure and serving marquee, plus the groundsman's house and vegetable garden behind the picket fence.

At right is Nevile Lodge's view of the beer tent and the test.

WITH SUCH A GLITTERING ARRAY OF TALENT, THE W. INDIES V. N.Z. TEST HAS EVERYTHING TO PROVIDE SCINTILLATING CRICKET—

SPARKLING BATTING BY THE WEST INDIANS —

BRILLIANT FIELDING BY THE NEW ZEALANDERS —

DAZZLING BOWLING FROM BOTH SIDES —

REFRESHMENTS

FOR THE FIRST TIME! LIQUOR ON SALE BEER ON TAP ALL SPIRITS AVAILABLE

AND UNDOUBTEDLY THE BRIGHTEST SPECTATORS EVER SEEN AT THE BASIN RESERVE

NEW ZEALAND CRICKET MUSEUM

TREVOR RIGBY COLLECTION

Playing or commentating at the Basin was always a thrill for Trevor Rigby (left). He was conscious of the prestige of the ground, even though the facilities during his playing days were uninviting, with changing rooms more like dungeons and showers more often than not cold.

Rigby first played at the ground as goalkeeper for the Rongotai College soccer First XI. They played some of their games on the No. 2 pitch at the same time as the 1949 Petone Settlers team were playing on the main ground in front of 10,000 spectators.

Rigby later played soccer for Miramar Rangers and cricket for Kilbirnie. For more than four decades, he experienced the ground first as a player, then as a radio commentator on both sports.

Soccer commentaries were initially made from a small room under the stairs at the northern end of the old stand. When there were big crowds, the commentators would use a stick to prod people to move them along if they were blocking the view. Cricket commentaries were broadcast from a small hutch alongside the sightscreen at the southern end, where the scoreboard is today.

Among the memories indelibly etched in Rigby's mind are:

- The six goals scored by John Donovan for Seatoun in a 7–1 win over Christchurch City in the 1958 Chatham Cup final.
- The regional final of the Chatham Cup in 1958, when Railways were leading 4–1 with eight minutes remaining and lost in extra time.
- The colourful Hungaria team that played a flowing imaginative style of soccer during the 1960s and drew an impressive local following.
- Richard Collinge bowling Geoff Boycott at the start of England's second innings in the test in 1978. Rigby says, with typical modesty, it is the only incident on which he commentated that is still in the archives.

◀ The Sisters of Mercy (Home of Compassion) ran a soup kitchen in Sussex Street for the unfortunates of Wellington. Many of their customers were alcoholics who, after their evening meal, would stand behind the cricketers at practice, offering sage advice. These people were called 'winos' by sportsmen and some slept out in the many nooks and crannies that were to be found at the Basin Reserve. This photo was taken at the northern end of the ground.

EVENING POST

The 1968–69 cricket season featured the fourth visit to New Zealand of an England women's team. At the Basin Reserve, New Zealand captain Trish McKelvey of Wellington became the first women's test centurion for New Zealand when she batted 332 minutes to compile 155 not out. England wicketkeeper Shirley Hodges admires another boundary through the off side. Until Jeremy Coney scored 174 not out against England in 1984, McKelvey held the New Zealand record for the highest test score at the Basin.

When she retired, McKelvey coached, selected and managed New Zealand women's teams. In 1992, she became the first woman to be a board member of the New Zealand Cricket Council.

After winning the Ashes series in Australia in 1970–71, Ray Illingworth's MCC side toured New Zealand. Wellington played the tourists in a 40-over match, the first limited-over game involving an international team in New Zealand. Before a capacity crowd, Wellington won by 23 runs. This was before the ozone layer became part of everyday usage or the Cancer Society initiated its 'Cover-up' campaign. Even sunhats were not part of standard cricket-watching attire.

Since its inception in 1923, the Chatham Cup had always featured a finalist from each of the North and South Islands. With the introduction of soccer's national league in 1970, the draw for the cup altered, and became open. In 1971, Western Suburbs of Wellington played Wellington City (an amalgamation of Miramar Rangers and Hungaria) on the first occasion that two teams from one island had met in the final. Ten players on the park had represented New Zealand. The game was played in a Wahine-type storm, with the wind howling from the north.

Paul Cameron, who played for Wellington City, recalls that the concrete bunker dressing rooms were as cold as ice and that in the wind players dispensed with limbering up because they struggled even to stand. Both sides adopted the tactic of shooting for goal from any range when playing with the wind, as the gale made it virtually impossible to string together passes.

Cameron followed the tactics to a T when he scored with a left-foot drive from the centre circle early in the game. All of the action was at the southern end of the ground, and some of the goal kicks even swirled behind for corners. Not one attacking shot was made at the northern end.

The score was 2–2 at fulltime. With the last kick of extra time, Barry Humphreys of Western Suburbs scored the winner when his cross from the eastern touchline bounced over the goalie and was blown into the net.

In the photo at right, Wellington City captain Grahame Bilby makes a save, watched by team-mates Alan Westwood and Jack Nathu. Bilby represented New Zealand at cricket and soccer, and never in 15 years of playing at the Basin Reserve did he experience a gale of such ferocity.

In 2001, the original Western Suburbs and City players staged a rematch to celebrate the only time two Wellington teams have met in the Chatham Cup final.

◀ Peter Whiting was one of the best goalkeepers produced by New Zealand. The big Wellingtonian played 14 times for New Zealand from 1961 to 1964 and helped Miramar Rangers win the 1966 Chatham Cup with a 1–0 victory over Western of Canterbury. Whiting was a regular at the Basin Reserve, where, apart from his club and international duties, he represented Wellington in domestic representative games and against touring sides from overseas. Whiting was a soccer pioneer – in 1966 he had a crack at playing the game professionally in England, playing 21 games for Charlton Athletic.

Whiting is keeping good company in this 1971 photo of Wellington taking on the touring Wolverhampton Wanderers team. His team-mate is Paul Cameron, another New Zealand representative, while the opposing forward is the brilliant Northern Ireland striker Derek Dougan, who scuttled Wellington's hopes by netting two goals. Wolves won the game 6–0.

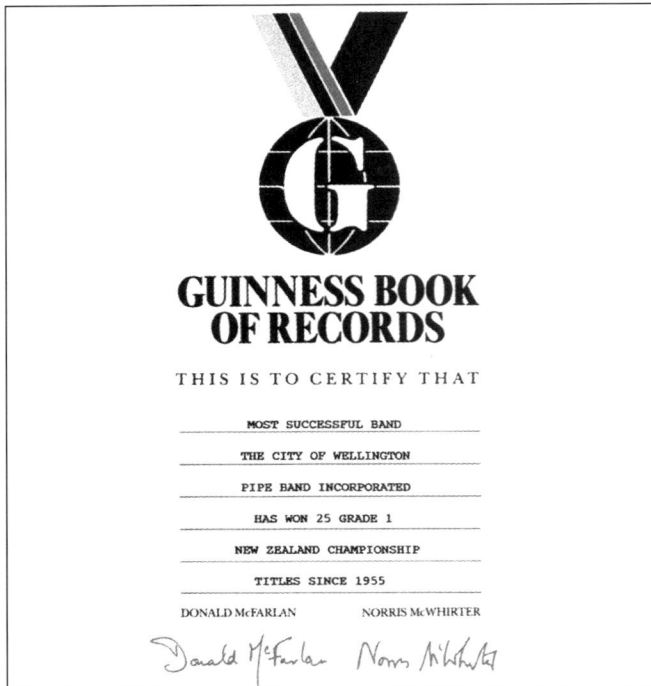

GUINNESS BOOK OF RECORDS

THIS IS TO CERTIFY THAT

MOST SUCCESSFUL BAND

THE CITY OF WELLINGTON

PIPE BAND INCORPORATED

HAS WON 25 GRADE 1

NEW ZEALAND CHAMPIONSHIP

TITLES SINCE 1955

DONALD McFARLAN   NORRIS McWHIRTER

The City of Wellington Highland Pipe Band was created at the end of the Second World War and used facilities in the bowels of the Basin Reserve grandstand, based in an area that by 2003 had become the archives storage room for the New Zealand Cricket Museum. This was to be the band's practice area until 1970. Cricketers changing after nets were accompanied to their showers by the wailing of practice chanters and drum rolls.

The growing band financed its operations by having crayfish suppers in the grandstand. During these, two sacks of crayfish and two sacks of potatoes were eaten as guests chanced their luck on games of chance into the small hours of the morning.

The band even made its way into the 1990 edition of the *Guinness Book of Records*, having won 25 grade-one New Zealand championships in 34 years. It is the most famous club, team or band in the long history of the Basin Reserve. Strangely, though it had a close association with the grandstand, the pipe band rarely performed on the ground.

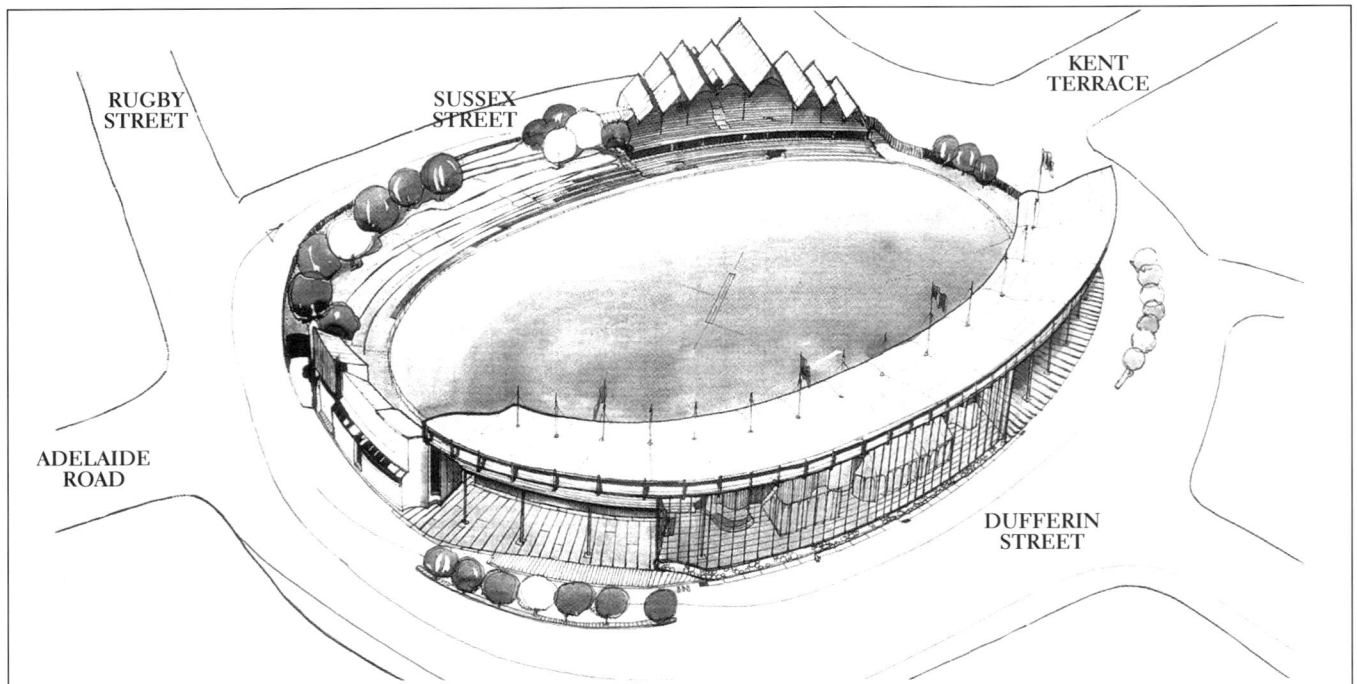

The *Evening Post* of 9 August 1974 announced a $4 million plan to turn the Basin Reserve into a versatile sports arena. The three-stage plan involved the complete reconstruction of the ground, with all existing facilities demolished and the provision for two stands and terraces to cater for up to 25,000 people. Features were:
- A stand at the northern end to seat 2,500 spectators directly behind the resited cricket block, which would run true north–south.
- The ground's shape to become oval.
- A public stand facing the sun on the eastern side, accommodating 10,000. It was envisaged it would have bars, restaurants and areas for indoor sports and cultural activities.
- A landscaped hill to be built on the western side, with 250 car parks underneath.

The designer, Bill Lovell-Smith, was warmly congratulated on his concept.

GRANT TILLY

During the 1970s, the *Evening Post* ran a series entitled 'Cityscapes', with sketches by Grant Tilly and words by David McGill. The Basin Reserve groundsman's shed featured in October 1976. The shed had originally been sited in the middle of the ground on the southern side, before being moved to its current site in 1915.

Marching continued to prosper in New Zealand, nowhere more so than in Wellington, where the local Lochiel team carried all before them. Wellington had had champion teams before – notably the Sargettes. But Lochiel raised marching to new levels, winning the national title nine times from 1966 to 1979. Instructor Colleen Pobar was a key figure in Lochiel's development, for it was her drive and knowledge in the mid-1960s that turned Lochiel into a champion team.

Lochiel marched in Australia in 1975 and, in 1978, became the first New Zealand team to perform at the Edinburgh Military Tattoo. They were to return there in 1983. Besides Pobar, other leading Lochiel figures have been Christine Knox (née McKone), Shona Adamson, Christine Hatfield, Jodene Tuau and Margaret Pearson.

The start of a dynasty – Lochiel, 1966. From left: Erin Boyd, Joy Burton, Wendy Thompson, Shona Adamson (née Robertson), Victoria Puddle, Virginia Gamble, Sharon O'Sullivan, Frances Kirk, Yvonne Burns, Margaret Cobham (née Pearson), leader.

COLLEEN POBAR COLLECTION

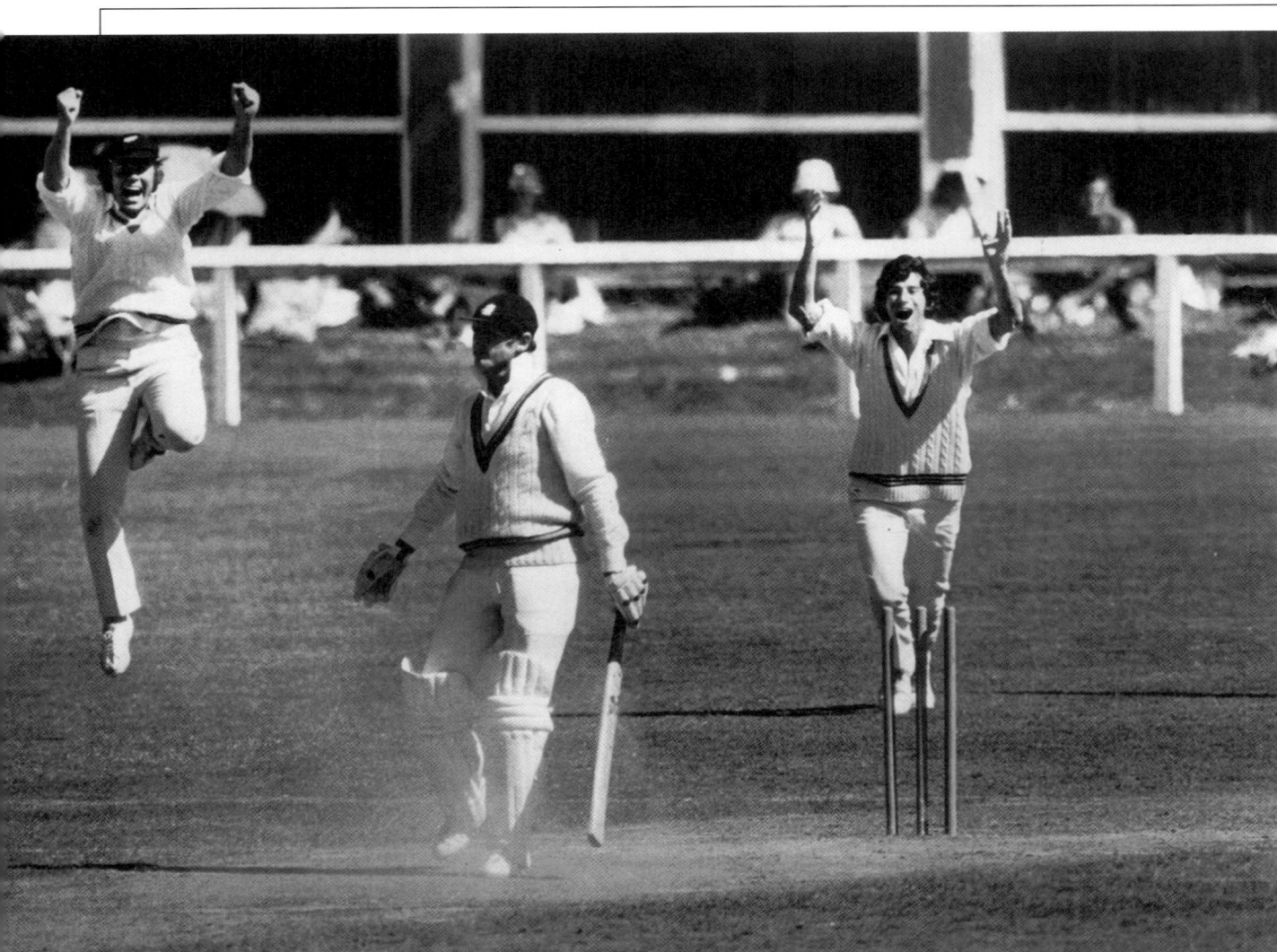

Richard Hadlee's wicket-taking test performances at the Basin Reserve against India in February 1976, when he captured 7–23 in the second innings, and against England in February 1978, when he had match figures of 10–100, became part of New Zealand cricket heritage.

Both games were won, but the victory against England gave the ultimate satisfaction. It was the 48th test New Zealand had played against England in 48 years and their first win over their oldest foe.

The first three days were played in a spiteful northerly. On the fourth day, the sun shone and in the last four hours, 17 wickets fell for only 101 runs. England, requiring a modest 137 runs for victory, got off to a nightmare start (as pictured above) when their best batsman, Geoff Boycott, was bowled by the fourth ball of Richard Collinge's first over, to the obvious delight of Robert Anderson (left) and Richard Hadlee. Many nominate that moment as the most significant in the Basin's cricket history.

Boycott's demise was so sudden it caught napping even some wise old heads. Dick Brittenden, Don Cameron and Alex Veysey, the three senior New Zealand cricket writers, had adjourned for an ale between innings and had not returned to their typewriters when they heard the cheering that signalled the dismissal.

Adding to the jubilant atmosphere was a blaring claxon that was sounded in a car yard across the road from the Basin in Dufferin Street.

England were dismissed for 64 before lunch on the fifth day and history was made. It was a fitting end for the old Basin. This was the last test played on the rectangular ground. Over the next three years, the ground was refashioned into an oval.

Rob Vance (right) was the driving force behind the refurbished Basin Reserve and it was most appropriate that to honour his services to cricket in Wellington and New Zealand the new stand was named the R. A. Vance Stand.

Vance played 44 games for Wellington from 1949 to 1962 and was a right-hand batsman who filled any of the top four positions in the order. He captained Wellington in 1953 and again in 1962.

Unusually, he became involved in administration while still a leading player. He joined the Wellington Cricket Association's management committee in 1952 and served on it until 1971. In 1958, he was elected chairman of the management committee and he filled this role for the next 13 years. He was elected a life member of the Wellington Cricket Association in 1971 and from 1991 to 1994 was the patron of Wellington Cricket.

Vance joined the New Zealand Cricket Council's management committee in 1966 and served for 11 years, before being made chairman in 1978, a position he filled with distinction for 10 years. He became a life member of New Zealand Cricket in 1988. There were other honours, including a CBE in 1982 and being made an Honorary Life Member of the MCC in 1984.

A little-known fact about the highly successful World Cup held in Australia and New Zealand in 1992 is that it originated with Rob Vance. In June 1987, he put his ideas on a jointly run competition to Australian officials at an ICC meeting in London. Initially they were cool to the idea, but their hesitation turned to enthusiasm five months later when Australia won the World Cup in India.

Vance was extremely well known in Wellington business circles as well, as for many years he was one of the principals of Vance Vivian, a busy menswear shop that was located on the corner of Manners Street and Cuba Street.

His son, also named Robert, was a top-order batsman who played in 119 first-class matches for Wellington from 1976 to 1991, second only to his long-time team-mate Evan Gray. Vance represented New Zealand over a two-year span, 1988–90, appearing in eight test matches and eight one-day internationals.

The refurbishing of the entire Basin Reserve has been a longstanding ambition of Wellingtonians and is now realised.

This historic and unique ground in the centre of the City is now blessed with a sense of enclosure, not only with the new stand but with the grass mounding to the east and south.

The design concept originated with the late Bill Lovell-Smith and his colleagues and has been furthered by the undoubted contribution of our Parks & Recreation Department. The realignment of the ground has brought the field much closer to the old stand which, for so many years, was remotely distanced from the scene of action, and the realignment of the wicket on a northwest, southeast axis greatly advantages both cricketers and spectators.

The Council has spared no effort to create of the Basin Reserve a venue which is unsurpassed in Australasia for cricket, soccer and other open air occasions and the new stand is the focal point of this enterprise. This boldly shaped and excellently sited facility, containing cricket practice wickets, splendid amenity rooms and 2000 covered seats is the envy of many cities and is a symbol of the Council's belief in the future of organised sport and the Basin Reserve.

We had little hesitation in proposing that the pavilion be known as the R.A. Vance Stand because Rob Vance has been not only a great cricketer and cricket administrator but also consistently behind the development and upgrading of this facility and is a most respected Wellingtonian.

30/9/80

MAYOR

The Midland Cricket Club, formed in 1883, always regarded the Basin as its home and had long dreamt of having clubrooms at the ground. Various city hotel bars and some of the uninviting rooms in the grandstand served until 1976, by which time Midland had amalgamated with St Patrick's Old Boys. In that year, permission was granted by the city council for clubrooms to be built in front of the groundsman's house, as seen in the photo at left, taken during the annual match between St Patrick's College and St Patrick's Silverstream in 1978. The photo also shows one of the four light towers that were in each corner of the ground. The St Patrick's tower looks down on the scene.

Within three years they were all gone. The groundsman's house and the tower had been demolished, St Patrick's College had moved to Kilbirnie, and the clubrooms had moved to the play area, where they are today the Sir Ron Brierley Pavilion, headquarters of Cricket Wellington.

The foundations of the new stand take shape in April 1979.

With work about to begin on reconstruction of the Basin, plans for the scoreboard, a contentious issue that had always blighted the venue, were revealed.

Designed by Bill Lovell-Smith, it presented an impressive amount of information. It showed the batsmen's totals in both innings, with bowling analysis featuring in the centre. A top panel that contained the not out batsmen's scores, extras, overs and team total would be operated by the scorers with the push of a button.

In 1977, the city council learned that it did not need $400,000 budgeted for its bus service and instead poured the money into the Basin Reserve fund, enabling work to begin in August 1978. This was ironic because for decades most plans to use the Basin for something other than sport had been made in the name of better transport.

Changes were made to Lovell-Smith's original plan. The eastern side of the oval became a tree-covered semicircular mound. The old grandstand was retained and the oval moved 20 metres closer to it. A picket fence was to enclose the playing area and a promenade built behind it. New terraces were to be built in front of the old stand.

▲ Sponsor Cable Price Downer's chief executive Bill Steele holds the model scoreboard. With him is Wellington mayor Michael Fowler and Rob Vance, chairman of the New Zealand Cricket Council.

▼ The distinctive roof-line of the R. A. Vance Stand appears in this photograph, taken in December 1979.

The new Basin Reserve hosted its first test in three years against India in February 1981. New Zealand had just been involved in a World Series Cricket limited-over tournament in Australia that completely changed the public face of cricket. Live television brought all the trappings of the modern game into New Zealanders' living rooms. Gladiatorial confrontations took place under lights in coloured clothing. White balls, black sightscreens and microphones spouting like mushrooms between the stumps added to the novelty.

Geoff Howarth's New Zealand team qualified to play Australia in the best-of-five final. The first two finals

matches were split and in the third, at Melbourne, there was the underarm incident when Trevor Chappell delivered the last ball of the game underarm to New Zealand number 10 Brian McKechnie to prevent him from having the opportunity to hit a six and tie the match. The incident caused a sensation, with even Prime Minister Rob Muldoon criticising the Australians' sportsmanship. Though they lost the final, the New Zealand team returned as superstars and public interest was at an all-time high.

The New Zealand players, the Indians and public gave the $2 million Basin restoration warm approval.

EIGHT

The Professional Age
1982–2003

CRICKET HAD NEVER dominated sport at the Basin Reserve as it has done since 1981. Other sports have had their days in the sun (or the wind, or the rain), but as Wellington has been increasingly served by good sports facilities, including the Westpac Stadium, the Mount Albert hockey complex, Queens Wharf Events Centre and Newtown Park, there have been fewer requirements for them to use the Basin.

More obviously than ever, the modern Basin is a cricket ground. The massive refurbishments that took place from 1978 to 1981 turned it from a rectangle into a cricket oval, and designer Bill Lovell-Smith ensured that the ground, while offering all the modern facilities and accoutrements of an international cricket ground, retained elements of the atmosphere of a quaint village green. This was quite some feat, considering the Basin has traffic pouring all around it and is only a short distance from the heart of downtown Wellington.

The upgrading of the Basin resulted in the imposing R. A. Vance Stand (which also contains an indoor cricket facility) in the north-west corner, the new scoreboard at the southern end, a reshaping of the ground and the building of an embankment on the western side. The cricketers have responded well to the changes, and there

The number of non-sports events held at the Basin has decreased. One exception was the big military tattoo during early December 1985. It was blessed with calm weather, judging by the limp flags, and more lighting than was normal for evening events.

EVENING POST

The city council's director of parks, Ian Galloway, expressed concern that the roof of the old stand was unsafe in excessively high winds. It was felt there was a threat of tiles and bolts flying off, and the stand was closed. The roof was replaced during the winter of 1984.

have been some magnificent games – both one-dayers and tests – played there over the past two decades.

Besides cricket, other sports visited the Basin, if only briefly. Australian Rules dipped its toe in the water in 1998, with encouraging results.

The last marching contest of any note held at the Basin took place during Labour Weekend 1995, when Wellington hosted the International Challenge between Australia and New Zealand. The weekend also marked New Zealand Marching's 50th anniversary. A highlight was the March of the Decades, which was broken into five-year segments. This display of marches, covering the past half-century of drill marching, was performed by former members of Lochiel, who had come together for the occasion. On the closing day, a spectacular massed drill of more than 200 marchers performed 28 detailed moves to the command of the whistle.

Lochiel won the International Challenge title and Champion Instructor went to Colleen Pobar. This celebration of marching drew crowds of nearly 10,000, but in a sense was a slightly sad occasion because it marked the end of marching's long association with the Basin Reserve. The last New Zealand championship at the ground was in 1983. These days the marchers go elsewhere to hold their big events, as they can no longer afford to use the Basin.

Rugby league generally shied away from the Basin.

There were exceptions – notably the Wellington v. Great Britain encounter in 1990 and a couple of big domestic representative fixtures. Rugby union returned to the Basin in the late 1990s when senior club games were played at the ground.

Soccer continued to use the Basin on occasion, but the ground no longer justified its tag as the Wembley of New Zealand. The All Whites, captained by Duncan Cole, drew 2–2 with Newcastle United in 1985, and in 1990 New Zealand scored a good 2–1 win over Moscow Locomotiv. But the Basin's biggest soccer international of the period was in 1992, when Wynton Rufer, New Zealand's greatest player, brokered a visit by his German club, Werder Bremen. On a chilly midwinter's day, the All Whites beat the German side 2–1 in front of a standing-room-only crowd.

The Chatham Cup final did not go to the Basin as a matter of course, though the ground continued to host finals as late as 1992, when Miramar Rangers gladdened local hearts by beating Waikato United 3–1.

▶ This aerial photo illustrates why the Basin has been termed the world's largest roundabout. The oval playing area is 150 metres wide through the centre of the cricket block, which is 24 metres wide and 35 metres long and can accommodate nine pitches.

There was some entertaining national league soccer played at the Basin over the years. Wellington's teams in the league in this period included Wellington Diamond United, Miramar Rangers, Waterside Karori and Wellington United. Hutt Valley United played the odd game on the Basin, when meeting a Wellington side.

But cricket has been the major sports focus. Martin Crowe made 299 against Sri Lanka in 1991 and with Andrew Jones, who made 186, added a world record 467 runs for the third wicket. Other leading New Zealand cricketers who performed with distinction in test matches at the Basin Reserve include Richard Hadlee, Ewen Chatfield, Jeremy Coney, Lance Cairns, Ken Rutherford, John Bracewell, Danny Morrison, John Wright, Nathan Astle, Craig McMillan, Matthew Sinclair,

A disturbing feature of the record crowds was the growing boorishness of some spectators. At the beginning of a day's play, slogans, banners and attire more in keeping with a pop concert created a splendid atmosphere. This was enhanced when spectators were allowed onto the field during the lunch interval. Unfortunately, shabby behaviour by a few somewhat inebriated watchers caused administrators concern later in the day.

Simon Doull, Chris Cairns, Stephen Fleming, Shane Bond and Mark Richardson.

The New Zealand test team, unbeaten in a home series through the 1980s, were especially formidable at the Basin, and have responded well to the recent concept of the Boxing Day test, giving local fans, who turn out in large numbers, plenty to cheer about. For four successive seasons, up to and including 2001–02, the Basin hosted two test matches a year. Except perhaps for Lord's, this is unique among test grounds of the world.

Some of the one-day internationals have been equally memorable. In the early 1980s, when the New Zealand team was really riding high, players like Lance Cairns, Glenn Turner and Bruce Edgar played big parts before sellout crowds. Over the years, Wellington's own Gavin Larsen became a crowd favourite. Martin Crowe, quite apart from hitting five test centuries on the Basin, played brilliantly in one-day matches. In 1990–91, Crowe opened the batting for Wellington with Richard Reid in the domestic Shell Cup competition and so breathtaking was their batting that they attracted thousands of extra spectators.

Cricket drew some high-profile visitors to the Basin. In 1997, built around the test against England, there was a reunion of the players of the 1946 Australia v. New Zealand test. Also attending were Lord Ian MacLaurin, chairman of the England and Wales Cricket Board (ECB), Tim Lamb, chief executive of the ECB, Colin Ingelby-MacKenzie, president of the MCC, Roger Knight, secretary of the MCC, Denis Rogers, chairman of the Australian Cricket Board, and Malcolm Gray, the chief executive of the Australian Cricket Board. Two years later, the 1949 New Zealand team to England had their 50th reunion during the South Africa test at the Basin and were invited to Government House, where they had a special audience with Princess Anne.

It has been a significant era for cricket, too, because Wellington Cricket celebrated its 125th anniversary in 2001. It is the oldest sports body in New Zealand.

One of the brightest pieces of news for the Basin came off the field. In 1998, the ground was declared a National Heritage Place, the first sports ground to be so named.

Early in the 1990s, it became clear that Athletic Park had had its day and was no longer a satisfactory venue for top rugby. The cost of restoring the ground was prohibitive. In 1991, the firm Architectural Workshop produced a plan that would provide seating for 28,000 at the Basin. It added that if the ground became a covered superbowl, 35,000 could be accommodated.

Three days before the All Blacks beat the Springboks 41–20 at the
WestpacTrust Stadium on 20 July 2002, they practised at the Basin Reserve.

In 1993, the mayor of Wellington, Fran Wilde, speaking at the Wellington Sportsperson of the Year awards, said, 'A city of this size cannot support two major venues. In developing the Basin, we're looking to provide a flexible 365-days-a-year, day-night venue available to a mixture of codes and with adequate high-quality seating, facilities, administration and hospitality space to make it a top-class venue.'

A year later, other sites were being touted, including railway wasteland on Aotea Quay. Sites at Porirua, Upper and Lower Hutt were also mentioned. Finally, agreement was reached and the current Westpac Stadium was developed on Aotea Quay.

It was projected that all test and one-day internationals would be played at the stadium. But they weren't, and after two years it became obvious that tests would be played at the Basin and one-day internationals at the stadium, with both grounds under the control of the Wellington Regional Stadium Trust.

It transpired that all-year-round, multi-purpose stadiums were not conducive to Wellington weather and the desires of the public.

▶ Football of a different kind was played at the Basin on 1 March 1998. An Australian Rules match was played between the Melbourne Demons and the Sydney Swans, as part of the Australian Cup competition. The Demons won 15.15 (105) to 14.9 (93), and a crowd of 8,000 thoroughly enjoyed the spectacle.

AGENDA

In December 1988, the city council approved a request by the Wellington Cricket Association to name the entrance gates after two famous Wellington players, thus generating greater interest and character for the ground. The northern entrance became the C. S. Dempster Gate, and that at the southern end became the J. R. Reid Gate.
DON NEELY COLLECTION

DON NEELY COLLECTION

New Zealand's winning a test series for the first time against England was born from defence, led by Jeremy Coney and Martin Crowe, in the second innings of the first test in the 1984 series.

England led on the first innings by 244 runs. Even with Crowe making his first test century, New Zealand started the final day only 91 runs in front and seven second innings wickets down. In perfect conditions, Coney took his overnight score from 76 to 174 not out by the time New Zealand's match-saving innings ended at 537. Coney's innings occupied eight hours. He left the field like a modern-day Pied Piper, surrounded by admiring children. New Zealand won the second test and drew the third to win the series 1–0.

With the player and entertainment facilities now based in the R. A. Vance Stand, the luncheon area and players' dressing rooms in the old grandstand fell into disrepair. The Wellington Umpires Association used the tearoom for their weekly meetings. One of their number, Stanley Cowman, had over the years accumulated a collection of cricket memorabilia. During the test between Australia and New Zealand in February 1986, he borrowed some trestles and magazine stands and, with the help of umpiring colleagues, laid out the material.

The game was interrupted by rain, and large numbers of the public came through the 'temporary museum'. John Oakley, the president of New Zealand Cricket, was so impressed that he determined, along with the then executive director of Wellington Cricket, Darran Hannah, and Cowman, that a permanent museum should arise from the derelict tearoom.

More than $100,000 was raised and under the direction of museum designer Gary Couchman, the National Cricket Museum was opened by the patron of the NZCC, the Governor-General, Sir Paul Reeves, on 29 November 1987.

Included in the collection is the third-oldest bat in the world, the Addington bat (right), which dates back to 1743. Cowman was the curator until his death in February 2003.

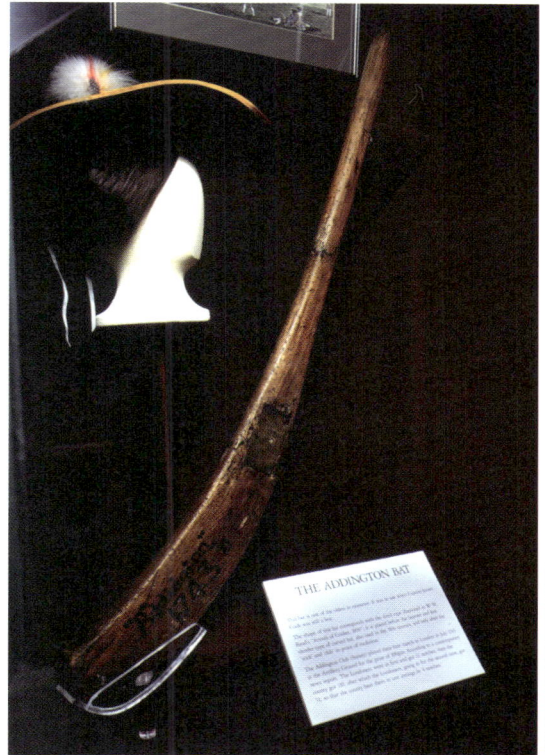

THE ADDINGTON BAT

NEW ZEALAND CRICKET MUSEUM

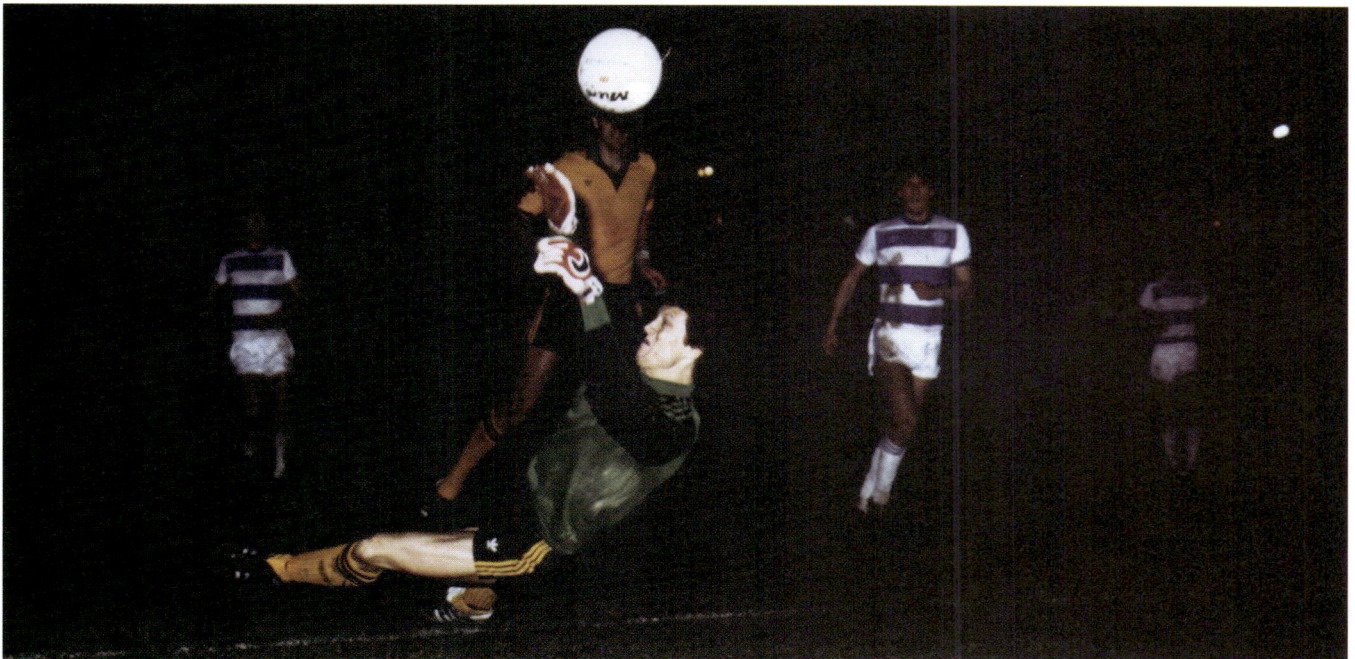

STEVE STEVENS

Night soccer was played regularly at the Basin Reserve from 1954. With the reconstruction of the Basin, the four banks of lights that were in each corner were reduced to three – one bank was removed from behind the R. A. Vance Stand. The lights were facetiously referred to as 'candle-power' by many players, some of whom compared night sport at the Basin to playing hide-and-seek. This photo of Wellington goalie Barry Pickering saving a shot from visiting English club side Queen's Park Rangers in – 1983 – emphasises the problem. The visitors, in the blue and white striped jerseys, are almost indistinguishable even 10 metres away.

In 1949, Sir Charles Norwood, a past mayor of Wellington and a successful businessman, established a trust fund that enabled five trophies to be awarded to the outstanding cricketers in Wellington, and in 1961 added another for captaincy. The beautifully crafted pewter and wood trophies have been treasured by the recipients ever since.

Sir Walter Norwood, Sir Charles's son, was equally devoted to cricket, and in 1971 his company, the New Zealand Motor Corporation, sponsored the first inter-provincial limited-over competition and continued to do so for the next six years.

A new dimension was added to New Zealand cricket when the R. A. Vance Stand opened and a substantial area was set aside for the entertainment of visiting officials, local dignitaries, administrators and former players. This area was named the Norwood Room, where a hundred guests enjoy the best view of cricket offered at any international ground in the world. Patrons view the cricket over the top of the sightscreen at the northern end of the ground and are only about 20 metres from the boundary.

The Norwood Trust has distributed more than $1 million to all sectors of cricket in the Wellington region. Sir Charles and Sir Walter have been key figures in the development of cricket in the area, so it is fitting that the Basin Reserve, Wellington's home of cricket, has such a prime area named in their honour.

ALEXANDER TURNBULL LIBRARY

▲ Sir Charles Norwood (left) and his son, Walter, later Sir Walter, pictured in 1928.

▼ A view of the Basin Reserve looking south from the Norwood Room of the R. A. Vance Stand.

DON NEELY COLLECTION

Wellington enjoyed some notable successes in the 1980s, which could well be termed a second golden era for the capital's cricket team (following the late 1920s to the early 1930s). Wellington won the Shell Trophy four times and the Shell Cup twice in this period.

Above is the Wellington team that won the Shell Trophy in the 1982–83 season. Standing, from left: John Gibson (selector), Peter Holland, Evan Gray, Ewen Chatfield, Brian Cederwall, Steve Maguiness, Ross Ormiston, Erv McSweeney, Tony Pigott. Seated: Mike Curtis (selector), Ian Dee (manager), Bert Vance, John Morrison (captain-selector), Jeremy Coney, Bruce Edgar.

Six members of this team played 165 tests between them and seven members played 320 one-day internationals. They played positive, winning cricket.

Note the woven sightscreen.

One of the enduring personalities at the Basin Reserve was an elderly bespectacled gentleman who quietly sought out players new to first-class cricket, seeking particulars of their birth, school background, etc. This person was Arthur Carman, the father of New Zealand sports statisticians.

Carman was a dedicated historian and superb statistician. His involvement with cricket and rugby statistics endured 63 years until his death on 28 November 1982. He edited the *Cricket Almanack of New Zealand* from its inception in 1948 until 1982 and the *Rugby Almanack of New Zealand* from 1935 to 1982. Asked if he could swap one of his books for a century on any ground in the world, he nominated the Basin – the old windswept Basin had a special appeal for Carman.

His contribution to New Zealand cricket and rugby is as great as any test player's and it is appropriate that the area for the media at the top of the R. A. Vance Stand is called 'Carman's Corner'.

EVENING POST

Reflections casting doom two days before the first test between New Zealand and Sri Lanka from 31 January to 4 February 1991. The Basin looks like a tourist postcard normally associated with Lake Mathieson in Westland. The doom was unfounded – the test not only took place, but national and world batting records were created.

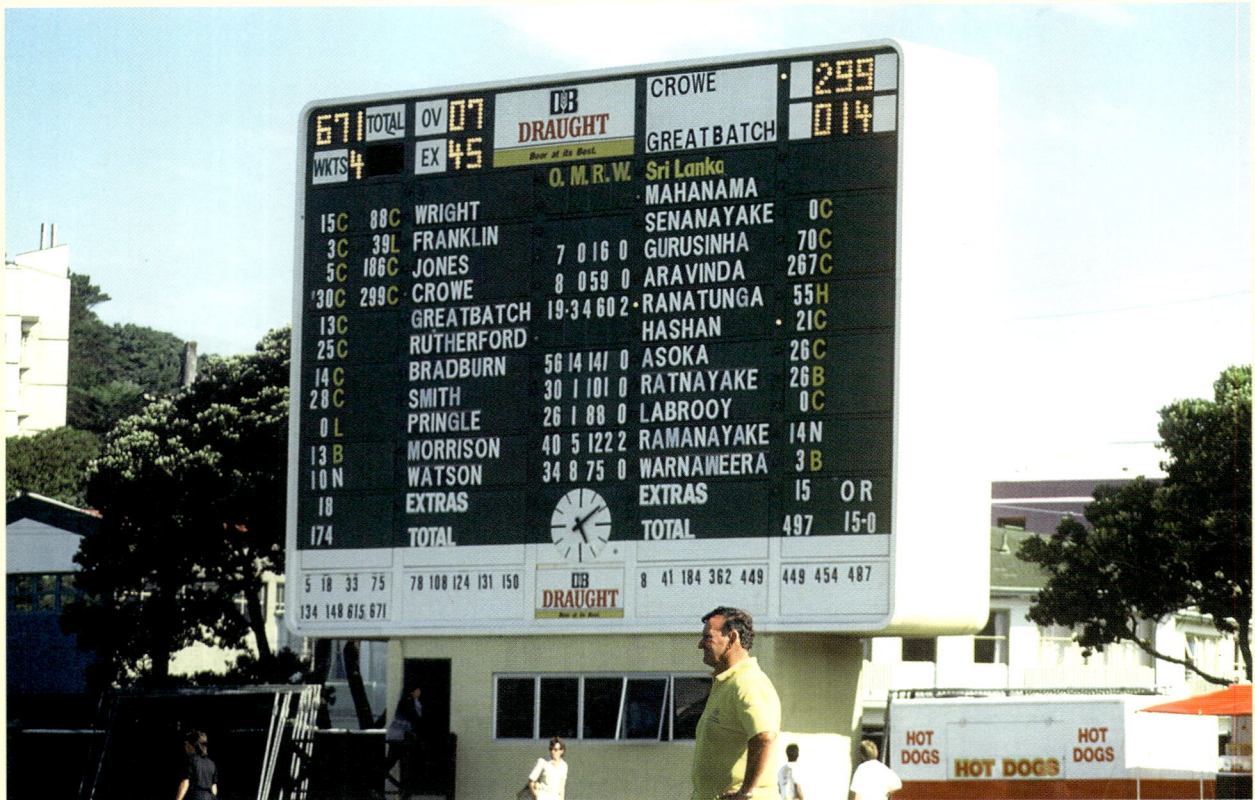

DON NEELY COLLECTION

Wes Armstrong is a contented man as he stands in front of the scoreboard after the record-breaking test. Armstrong succeeded Doug Kelly as groundsman at the Basin Reserve and held the post for more than 20 years, until Trevor Jackson took over. He was rightly proud that from 1969 to 1994 New Zealand remained unbeaten in their 18 tests at the Basin, winning six and drawing 12.

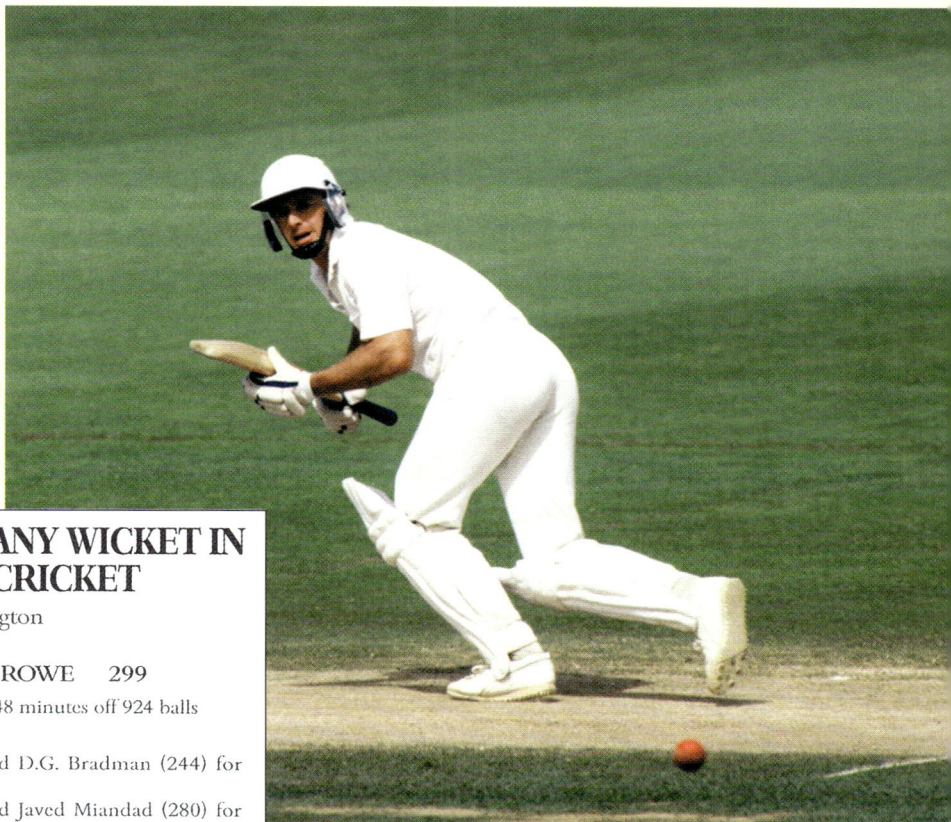

▲ **Andrew Jones**

▼ **Martin Crowe**

HIGHEST PARTNERSHIP FOR ANY WICKET IN THE HISTORY OF TEST CRICKET

at the Basin Reserve, Wellington
3, 4 February 1991

A.H. JONES   186   M.D. CROWE   299

- 467 for the 3rd wicket against Sri Lanka scored in 548 minutes off 924 balls

Previous best being:

- 451 for the 2nd wicket W.H. Ponsford (266) and D.G. Bradman (244) for Australia v England at the Oval, 1934

- 451 for the 3rd wicket Mudassar Nazar (231) and Javed Miandad (280) for Pakistan v India at Hyderabad, 1982-83.

WORLD RECORD

- 467 runs is the best-ever 3rd-wicket partnership in first-class cricket, beating the previous best of 456 by Khalid Irtiza (290) and Aslam Ali (236) United Bank v Multan at Karachi, Pakistan, 1975-76.

NEW ZEALAND TEST RECORDS

- 467 runs beat the previous partnership record of 367 scored by G.M. Turner (259) and T.W. Jarvis (182) v West Indies at Georgetown, Guyana, 1971-72.

- 299 runs to M.D. Crowe beat the previous highest test score by a New Zealander made in New Zealand of 239 by G.T. Dowling against India at Lancaster Park, Christchurch, 1967-68.

- New Zealand total of 671-4 is the highest team total beating 553-7 declared against Australia at Woolloongabba, Brisbane, 1985-86.

- M.D. Crowe's match aggregate of 329 beats the previous highest aggregate of 259 made by G.M. Turner v West Indies at Georgetown, Guyana, 1971-72.

NEW ZEALAND RECORD

- 467 runs is the highest first-class partnership for any wicket beating 445 made by W.N. Carson (290) and P.E. Whitelaw (195) for Auckland v Otago at Carisbrook, Dunedin, 1936-37.

BASIN RESERVE RECORD

- 299 runs to M.D. Crowe beats the previous highest score made on the ground in first-class cricket of 296 by J.R. Reid, Wellington v Northern Districts, 1962-63.

- 299 runs to M.D. Crowe beats the previous highest test score made on the ground of 267 by P.A. de Silva, Sri Lanka v New Zealand, 1990-91

- The New Zealand total of 671-4 is the highest team score beating 595 by Wellington v Auckland, 1927-28.

Two features of the one-day clash between Wellington and Northern Districts on 16 January 1989 were that admission was free, which resulted in an attendance of 6,000, and that at the lunch-break players from both teams sat at tables and signed autographs.

There was a magic rugby league moment at the Basin Reserve on Wednesday, 27 June 1990, when coach Howie Tamati's Wellington team recovered from a 22–8 halftime deficit to beat Great Britain 30–22. It was the first time Wellington had beaten an international side. Stars for Wellington included Mike Kuiti, Geoffrey Tangira, Morvin Edwards and left-winger Victor Aramoana, seen at right scoring the try that sealed the game. One of the big names in the visiting side was former Wales rugby union flyhalf Jonathon Davies.

By 1990, most big league games in the capital were played at the Petone Recreation Ground, for the strength of league by then had shifted to the Hutt Valley. However, it was hoped there would be a sizeable crowd for the Britain game and the Basin was chosen because of its bigger capacity. As it was, the weather was excellent and a good crowd turned out to watch an historic occasion.

Although the weather was fine, no play was possible because of the wet outfield
in Wellington's Shell Trophy fixture against Canterbury on 26 November 1992,
so the Westpac rescue helicopter was used to dry the ground.

PROPOSED THROUGH-TUNNEL UNDER BASIN RESERVE

PRECAST CONCRETE PIPE
READY TO BE LOWERED
INTO TRENCH

ADELAIDE RD

CAMBRIDGE TCE

KENT TCE

TO MT VICTORIA
TUNNEL

TRENCH CARVED THROUGH
THE HEART OF THE BASIN
RESERVE TO ACCOMMODATE
THROUGH-TRAFFIC TUNNEL

Once again the traffic bottleneck caused by vehicles
heading to the Mount Victoria tunnel was in the news.
Wellington City Councillor Brian Weyburne suggested
building a road tunnel from Adelaide Road under the
Basin Reserve using a huge concrete pipe that could be
inserted and then covered over 'and the Basin returned
to its pristine condition'. As with so many other propos-
als for the Basin down the years, it came to nothing.

163

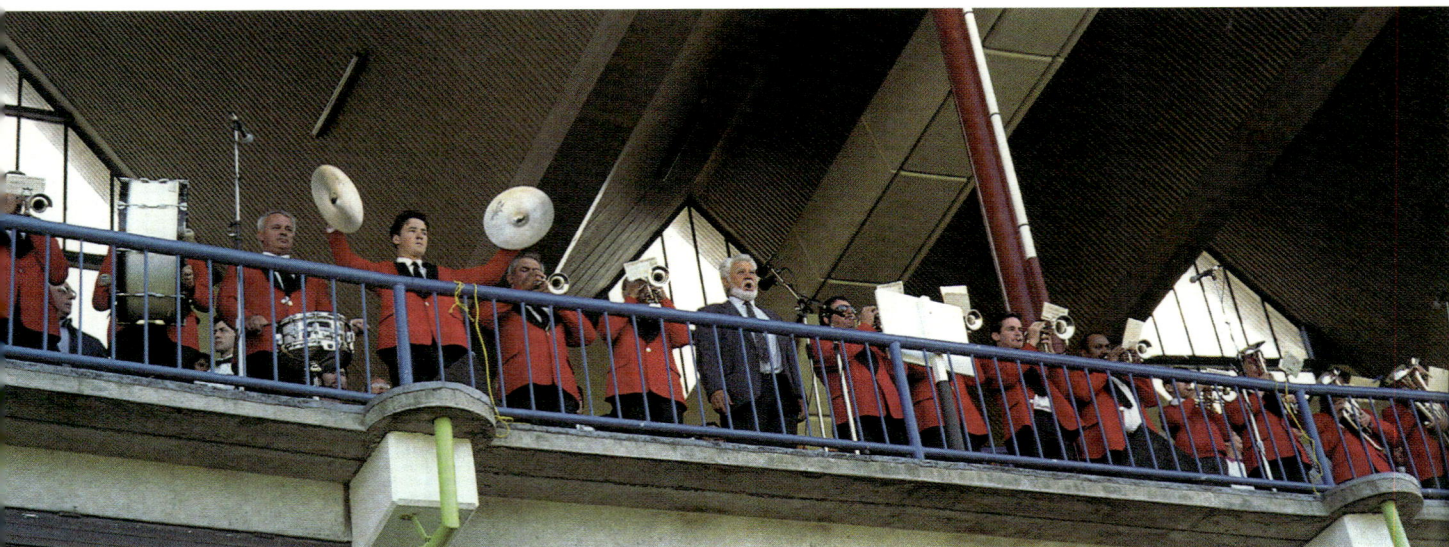

The fifth cricket World Cup was hosted by Australia and New Zealand in 1992 and with the late inclusion of South Africa, after two decades in the international cricket wilderness because of its apartheid laws, it was the first genuine World Cup.

The Basin Reserve hosted three games in March, including New Zealand's win over England by seven wickets with nine overs remaining, featuring fine batting by Martin Crowe and Andrew Jones.

The International Festival of the Arts was on in Wellington at the time, and Donald McIntyre, now Sir Donald, world-famous bass baritone, sang 'God Defend New Zealand', supported by the Evening Post Brass Band (above).

Russian club side Moscow Locomotiv FC played a three-match series against New Zealand in July 1990. Each side won a game after the first had been drawn. The All Whites won 2–1 at the Basin Reserve. Robert Ironside, first in white from the left, heads high this time, but he did score twice.

▲ For more than a quarter of a century, John Oakley has been a major contributor to cricket at the Basin Reserve. Because he had visited many of the world's major test venues, he had a vision of what should be done to make the ground truly international. The building of the New Zealand Cricket Museum and the Norwood Room have helped his vision become a reality and the Basin Reserve become the predominant test venue in New Zealand. Oakley and his good friend Sir Ron Brierley have been the driving forces behind the numerous reunions that have taken place during test matches.

From left, John Oakley entertains his South African friends Dr Ali Bacher (former test player, later chief executive of South Africa Cricket Board), Roy McLean (former test player), and Joe Pamensky (South Africa Cricket Board member) at the New Zealand Cricket Museum during the 1992 World Cup.

▶ The Basin, looking to the grandstands and the Carillon from the grassy bank.

▶ An evening with the New Zealand Symphony Orchestra on 4 December 1994 provided a stunning performance of Tchaikovsky's *1812 Overture*, played with live cannonfire, fireworks and the bells of the Carillon nearby. The Opera at the Basin also featured Dame Malvina Major, Australian tenor Edmund Barham and the band of the RNZAF. Concert-goers were asked to wear soft-soled flat shoes and bring cushions rather than chairs to protect the outfield. A giant video screen was also used. Note that the cricket square in the middle of the ground was covered.

▲ In February 1997, a belated reunion was held for the surviving members of New Zealand's first official test against Australia, at the Basin Reserve in 1946.

Survivors who attended the reunion were: back, from left: Eric Tindill, Len Butterfield, Walter Hadlee, Merv Wallace (all New Zealand). Front: Ian Johnson, Bill Brown, Keith Miller, Ron Hammence, Ernie Toshack, Ken Meuleman (all Australia).

The photos on the wall record New Zealand's test victories at the Basin Reserve.

▼ In 1999, Lindsay Weir, the sole survivor of the New Zealand team that played the first test on the Basin Reserve, in 1930, was a guest at the ground during the test against South Africa. During the game, he unveiled a large bronze plaque commemorating that historic game.

It was inset into the promenade near where the players take the field. Don Neely envisaged that all major historical moments at the Basin would eventually be recorded in this way, thus creating an informative walkway.

The famous 1949 New Zealand team to England – the Forty-Niners – held their 50-year reunion during the South Africa test.

The view from the commentary box high in the R. A. Vance Stand.

During the test against South Africa in 1999, the opportunity was taken to mark the 100th test match that radio commentator Bryan Waddle had covered. It was most apt that the presentation was made by the president of New Zealand Cricket, Iain Gallaway, who was his first mentor in cricket broadcasting.

As a youngster, Waddle grew up in a house dominated by the doings of the Karori Cricket Club, where his father, George, filled most roles from general dogsbody to scorer for the senior team, while his mother, Rita, was in charge of afternoon tea.

George Waddle was a real Wellington cricket identity in his own right. He was a member of the Wellington Cricket Association's management committee and was a long-serving ground announcer at the Basin. George was well known for playing the 'Invercargill March' over the loudspeaker to accompany teams as they walked out to field after the lunch or tea breaks, or after a change of innings.

Bryan went on to play senior cricket for Wellington College Old Boys and says playing on the Basin was always a special thrill, especially when he was on the No. 2 pitch, which was closest to the first-class wicket block.

When he joined broadcasting, Waddle worked alongside Trevor Rigby, Noel Lawson, Grant Nisbett, Bob Forsyth and Glyn Tucker in the small commentary box at the southern end. He was fortunate that, soon after he started doing reports and commentaries for commercial stations, the R. A. Vance stand opened with its state-of-the-art conditions for the media in the roofline of the stand.

Having broadcast more than 20 test matches from the Basin, Waddle still regards it as the best international cricket venue in the world because of its intimacy. He also enjoys being able to walk around the ground to soak up the game. Waddle is enamored of the Boxing Day test and regards it as an occasion that has captured the public imagination.

The WestpacTrust Stadium opened in
Wellington's Aotea Quay on 8 January 2000
with a one-day international between New
Zealand and the West Indies. Regrettably,
rain affected the grand occasion and only
10 overs were possible. The following day
the largest crowd ever assembled for a
cricket match in Wellington, more than
20,000, watched New Zealand win the
delayed match and enjoyed the qualities
of this stunning new sports complex.
Many remarked on the splendid lighting
and the giant replay screen was much
appreciated.

The advantages of Wellington's having
two international sports venues was
demonstrated during the cricket test against
England in March 2002 when, at the end
of the day's play, spectators could walk to
the WestpacTrust Stadium to watch the
Hurricanes play the Cats, from South
Africa, in the Super 12 rugby competition.

PETE BONNER

▲ In front of the imposing honours board in the Norwood Room stand some of the people whose names are recorded on it. From left: Malcolm McCaw (Wellington Cricket president 1985–87); John Oakley, CBE (Wellington life member, president 1982–85, New Zealand Cricket president 1985–87); Sir Ron Brierley (Wellington life member, president 1990–95, New Zealand president 1994–95); Rob Vance, CBE (Wellington life member, patron 1991–94, chairman 1958–71, New Zealand life member, chairman 1978–89); Mick Randall (Wellington president 1976–79); 'Jumbo' Symes (Wellington president 1971–74); Sir John Anderson, KBE, (Wellington president 1987–90, New Zealand chairman 1995–); Michael Horsley (Wellington chairman 1988–99).

▼ One of the great successes of Bill Lovell-Smith's design has been the eastern bank, with St Mark's Church in the background. It suggests a 'village green' atmosphere, besides providing sunny slopes for picnic lunches.

The introduction of a test on Boxing Day has been a notable success for Wellington and the Basin Reserve.

Spectator interest has been high and the games have been enhanced by the strategic placement of 58 pohutukawa trees encircling the ground, with up to 40 in full, majestic bloom. In four years of Boxing Day tests, New Zealand has beaten India, the West Indies and Bangladesh and drawn with Zimbabwe.

Since 1964, Wellington has had Ian Smith as its head scorer. During this time, he has scored in 29 tests at the Basin Reserve and has recorded victory for New Zealand there on 10 occasions.

When Smith began, scorers shared a box with the press on the eastern side, next to the scoreboard. Since the 'new' Basin opened in 1981, he has scored directly below the scoreboard, at the southern end.

Since 1983, Smith has been co-editor of the *New Zealand Cricket Almanack* with Francis Payne.

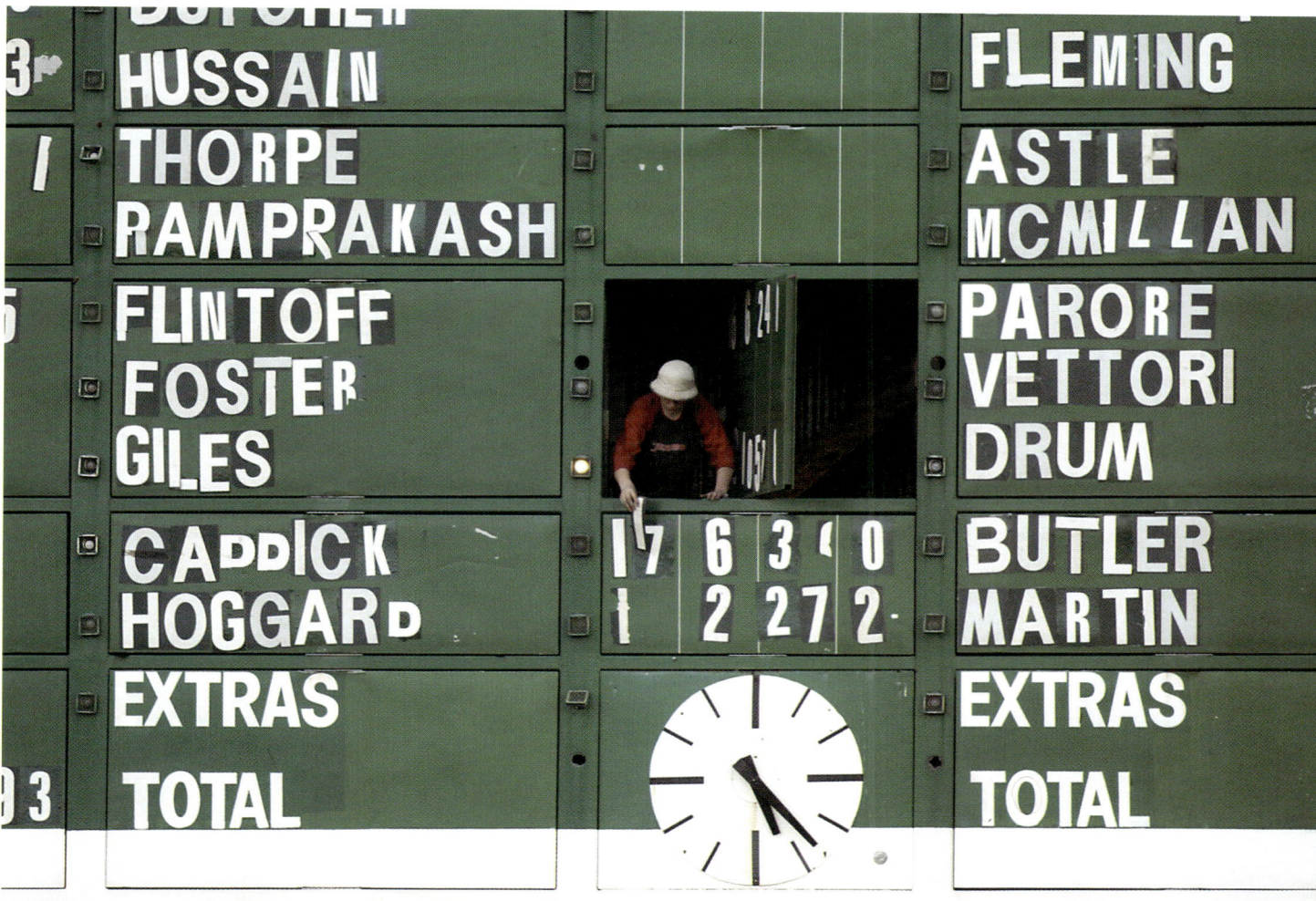

Commentator Jeremy Coney caused smiles when he described the Basin Reserve scoreboard during the 2002 test against England as 'looking like a ransom note'. A shortage of letters had been caused by strong winds blowing them off the board during the previous State matches.

A further 90 square metres was brought into the Cricket Museum in 2002. This enabled the addition of the John H. Oakley Gallery, an interactive room, a theatrette, an air-conditioning unit and a large storage room.

Since its opening, more than 300 packages, suit-cases and parcels have been sent to the museum for safe-keeping. The name of the museum was changed during 2002 to the New Zealand Cricket Museum, which better reflects the fact that it preserves and dis-plays the cricket treasures of the entire country, not just those pertaining to Wellington.

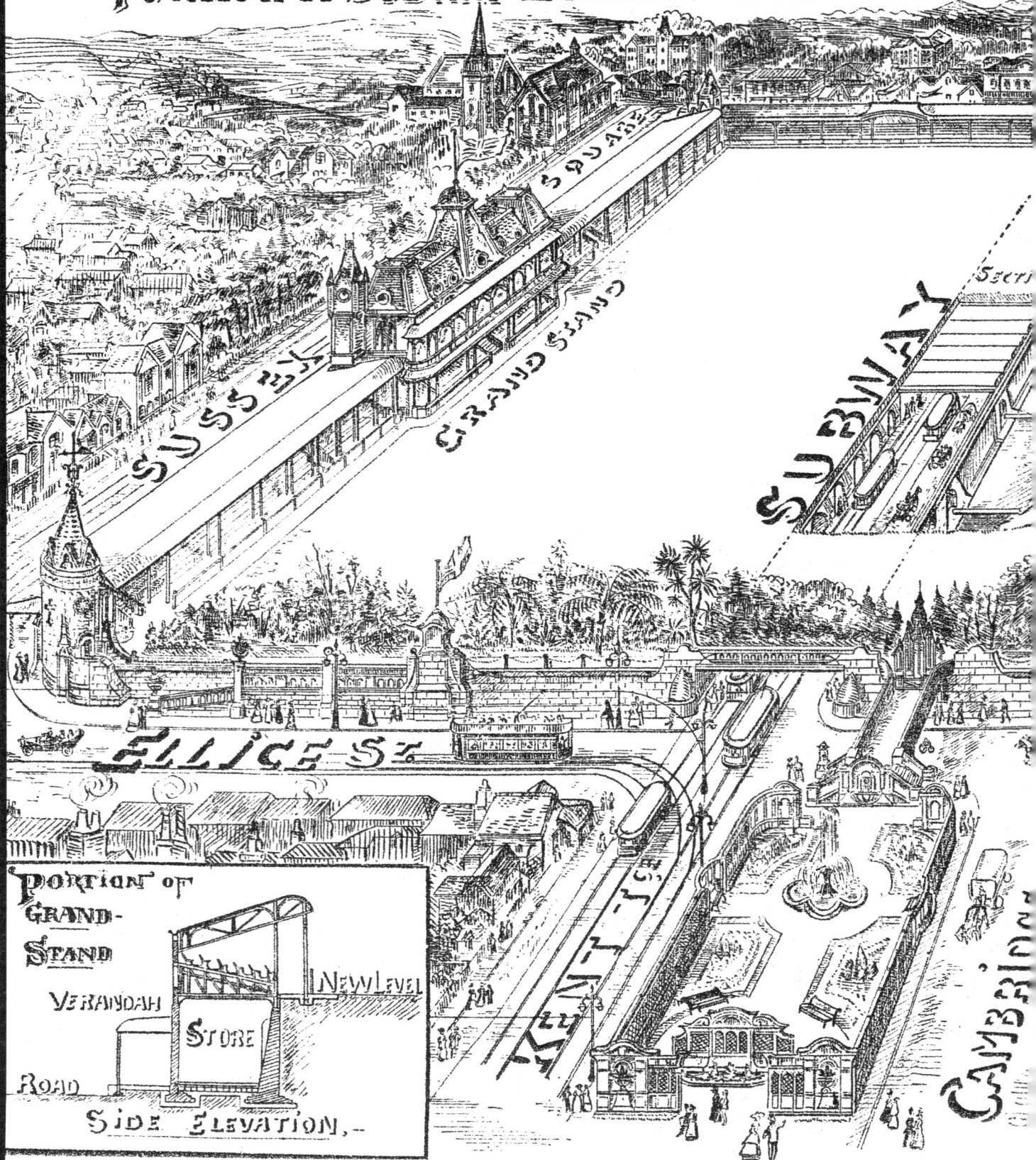

BASIN RESERVE IMPROVEMENT SC

TO ALLOW A SUBWAY BENEATH – PROVIDING FOR

SQUARE

SUSSEX

GRAND STAND

SUBWAY

Sect

ELLICE St.

KENT St.

CAMBRIDGE

PORTION OF GRAND-STAND

VERANDAH

STORE

NEW LEVEL

ROAD

SIDE ELEVATION.